D1358197

PRAISE FOR A.K. TURNER

"Empty bladder before reading."

– Laurie Notaro, *New York Times* bestselling author
of *The Idiot Girls' Action-Adventure Club*

This Little Piggy Went to the Liquor Store "candidly reveals
and revels in the flaws and dysfunctions of the author
and her family. Turner is not afraid to voice her private
thoughts and never takes herself too seriously...
refreshingly honest."

– *Publishers Weekly*

"Did Erma Bombeck ever guzzle vodka? If she did, she
might have come close to the ribald domestic humor in
Turner's 'momoir' *This Little Piggy Went to the Liquor Store.*"

– The Quivering Pen

"The perfect cross between Nora Ephron, David Sedaris,
and Chelsea Handler."

– Elaine Ambrose, *Menopause Sucks*

Mommy Had a Little Flask

A.K. Turner

FEVER STREAK PRESS

FEVER STREAK PRESS

Mommy Had a Little Flask
Copyright © 2013 A.K. Turner
All rights reserved.

ISBN: 978-0-9855839-8-9

Design by Sarah Tregay, DesignWorks, Inc.
Cover photo by Amaura Mitchell
Author photo by LeAna Earley

For my daughters and the women they will become.

CONTENTS

CHAPTER ONE

The Vice Squad

"Shaka-kahn, your mom!" Virgil stormed the kitchen. My brother-in-law is incapable of entering a house quietly. He has no knowledge of the custom of knocking, and he disregards typical greetings of "hello" or "hi, how are you?" in favor of his own salutation of "Shaka-kahn, your mom."

"Shaka-kahn, *your* mom," my husband, Mike, replied.

"You know," I said for the hundredth time, "you guys have the *same* mom." They ignored me.

"So, I got this new job," Virgil said.

"Lord, help us," muttered Mike, handing his brother a beer. Virgil is perpetually on the brink of losing a job, landing a job, getting a raise, or not getting paid. This latter event is a curious one to which only Virgil is prone. When he needs cash, it's not because he spent his money at a dive bar or got fired or failed to show up for work, it's because a boss inexplicably failed to pay him.

"And I mean, thank god I got fired from my old one," Virgil continued. As he spoke, he lifted up his shirt and caressed his large, hairy belly with both hands. "Well, I didn't really get fired, I quit, but that's great because my new job is awesome and comes with a huge raise. It's like crazy because there are these two other guys, but they don't know what the hell they're doing, and now I'm their supervisor. I just started today. Amanda, what's that smell?" This was the first time he addressed me directly, and I had a sudden flash of paranoia that all odors in my home were attributed solely to me.

"Jalapeños," I answered. "They'll be ready in five minutes." I'd been cultivating an addiction to stuffed jalapeños, which I justified because they are technically a *vegetable*. While I may stuff them with meat and cheese, they are still a vegetable stuffed with meat and cheese. My rationale is based on an important parenting technique that I like to call Willful Denial of Fact. It's the same logic I employ when telling myself that my kids eat healthily because I put cucumber slices on their plates, never mind the fact that they don't touch the cucumbers and only consume foods in the shapes of fish and dinosaurs. Willful Denial of Fact has other uses, as well. For instance, you can't tell me that I consumed an entire bottle of wine myself if the wine came out of a box.

"Virgil?" I asked. "Is it possible for you not to rub your big, furry stomach in my kitchen? It's a bit… distracting." I wanted to say "gross" but was trying to be kind. He mercifully lowered his shirt but continued running both hands over his middle.

"What's the new job?" Mike asked.

"I don't know, like cleaning up trash in an old crappy house, and then we'll rehab it. I'll start on Monday."

"I thought you said you started today," Mike said.

"No." Virgil shook his potbelly for emphasis, a signature move. "Do you even hear anything anyone else says? I said I'll start on *Monday*. Did you guys hear about the dude that got caught with the thing in his car?"

"What are you talking about?" I couldn't recall seeing a headline about a "dude" and his "thing."

"At least he didn't kill a monkey," he said. "*That* guy really screwed up. I mean, what kind of sick bastard kills a monkey?"

At the time, Boise held a collective anger toward a yet to be identified monkey killer. Someone broke into the Boise Zoo, was spotted by security but then evaded the police, and after all was said and done, a monkey was dead. Eventually the monkey killer would be arrested, and it turned out his aim was not to injure a monkey, but instead to *steal* a monkey. Perhaps he held an obsession with David Schwimmer's character on *Friends* and wanted a little Marcel of his own. As disturbing as his intention to steal the unfortunate creature was, the fact that he made it into the zoo at 4 a.m. and then into the monkey enclosure was even more troubling. Aren't the animal exhibits locked somehow? If an idiot who thinks that he can keep a stolen monkey as his pet can get into the cage, then surely a monkey, no doubt smarter than the aforementioned idiot, can get out. In any case, while attempting to remove the monkey from the zoo, the man got bit on the hand. Apparently monkeys don't like to be kidnapped and wrapped in people's coats. Especially by drunk people, which this idiot was. In response, the man beat the monkey on the head with a branch, and the monkey later died. Virgil's comment about the monkey was one of those rare instances when he says something completely off the wall, but I actually know what he's talking about.

"Let's not talk about the *demise* of the *primate*," I said, coding my language so that my daughters in the next room wouldn't overhear. We were frequent patrons of the zoo, and I wasn't yet ready to break the news. I'd also been (poorly) fielding many questions of late from my five-year-old, Emilia, about death in general. I was honest about the "Everybody dies" part, but then usually followed it up with "Who wants to go get some ice cream and pick out a new toy!" I wanted to have my thoughts in order and avoid this scenario before we tackled the monkey business. Otherwise, Emilia was likely to become obsessed with death once she figured out that conversations about it resulted in ice-cream cones and Barbie dolls.

"I'm going to smoke," Virgil said.

"No cigarette butts on the ground!" I commanded.

"Calm down, woman!" he yelled. "There's no need to yell. I clean up after myself."

I don't like to think of myself as someone who yells often, but in Virgil's case, it's fairly appropriate. Yelling as my primary means of communicating with Virgil has engendered in him an irrational fear of me. This fear, in turn, has resulted in a marked decline in the average number of times he asks me for money. Now he asks Mike for money. The last time he did this, about three months prior, Mike called me, and the conversation was as follows:

> Mike (with trepidation): "Amanda, I want to loan my brother some money."

I generally take the view that loaning money to Virgil is not a wise idea. However, Virgil is Mike's brother, and if he wants to loan money to him, I'm not going to interfere or question his decision.

Me: "Okay, what do you want me to do?"

Mike: "The power company won't turn his power back on until someone calls them and pays with a credit card. I'm driving, and I just can't take care of this right now."

This made me feel a little bit better about the situation. I'd rather the money go directly to the power company than to Virgil to take to the power company after a brief stop at a dive bar for a shot and a beer. And a shot and a beer and a beer and a beer.

Me: "I can call for you, but I'm assuming I'll need his account number and address." (Some might think it odd that I do not know Virgil's address or even in what neighborhood he resides, but I'm perfectly comfortable with this lack of information.)

Mike: "Yes, you'll have to get that from him."

Me: "Then why didn't he just call me himself?"

Mike: "I asked him to, but he's afraid of you."

Me: "Okay, that makes sense."

Virgil finished smoking and reentered the kitchen as I took the jalapeños from the oven. Mike's other sibling, Sandi, arrived.

"Chello, everyone," she greeted me and her brothers.

"What's up, Sister Christian," Virgil said.

"Are you actually getting shorter?" Mike asked.

"Let's hope not," she answered. "I don't have a lot to work with here." Sandi is four feet ten inches tall but compensates for her lack of height with endless energy and spunk. "But, you know, I've never really had a problem being short."

"That's good," said Virgil, "since you can't do shit about it."

Sandi ignored him and tried a jalapeño. "Ooh, nummers," she said. "That is some *nums*."

Nummers is one of those absolutely ridiculous fabricated baby-talk words that drive me insane. It's so cutesy and ridiculous that I hear it and find myself wanting to cause some sort of destruction. Like I want to find a flowerbed and trample it. I want to take something cute and make it not cute, because that's the reaction I have when a grown person, or anyone over the age of eighteen months, describes something as *nummers*. I think Sandi bears the initial responsibility for creating and using this horrible non-word, which should be universally banned, but other members of the Turner clan have since picked it up. I grit my teeth when anyone says *nummers*, especially in light of the fact that they are usually trying to pay me a compliment. *Did you mean to tell me that what I made was delicious or wonderful or excellent or even just good? Because I will take any of those over the word nummers.* But now, Sandi was creating new forms of what isn't even a word to begin with. Tacking on "that is some nums" was over-the-top unacceptable and a blight on the English language.

Another one that disturbed me, but that Sandi thankfully grew out of, was *wawa* for water. I understand that when a child learns to speak, "water" may come out as sounding more like "wawa." But that is no reason for the parent to then begin referring to water as *wawa*. It is the parent who is supposed to teach the child how to speak. The parent is not supposed to adopt the child's baby talk as the new and improved English. I also cringe at use of the word *binkie* or some other such cutesy and idiotic word for pacifier. It's a pacifier, plain and simple. Sure it's four syllables, but so is procreation. And if you are old enough to procreate and end up with a baby out of the deal, then you are old enough to say pacifier and delicious and water.

Maybe when your child is learning to talk and comes up with the substitute of *wawa* for water, you let it slip once or twice and ask them if they want some *wawa*. The correct course of action is to immediately reprimand yourself and vow never to make such a grievous error again. Not only did Sandi fail to reprimand herself as such when her daughters were tiny, but she continued to use the non-word of *wawa* long past when her children could say water. Seeing a grown adult ask a six-year-old if she wants *wawa* makes me want to call Child Protective Services.

"Sandi," I said, "I'm sorry, but I absolutely have to put my foot down. *Nummers* is not a word. *Nummers* has never been a word, and now you're bastardizing even that."

"What are you talking about? What did I say?"

"You said, 'That is some *nums*.'"

"So?"

"You just can't do that!"

At this point, my husband and his siblings rolled their eyes. Just as I feel I've spent years dealing with their butchered speech, they feel they've spent years dealing with my bitching about their butchered speech.

"Sure I can," said Sandi. "Why not?"

"Don't pay any attention to her," Virgil said. "It's just because she's a writer. She can't help it. She was born that way."

He turned to me then and said, "People are always so amazed when I tell them that your dad is Dean Koontz."

"You tell people what?" I asked.

"Isn't your dad a writer, too? I tell everyone your dad is Dean Koontz. You know, the guy who wrote *The Shining*."

"Wow," I said. "It would be pretty difficult for you to mess up that statement any worse than you just did." Suddenly *nummers* and *wawa* didn't seem so bad.

"Isn't your dad a writer?"

"Yes."

"But your dad isn't Dean Koontz?" He looked perplexed, as if there was one male writer on the earth named Dean Koontz, and he'd written one book called *The Shining*. So if my father was a writer, in Virgil's mind he must be *that* guy.

"I feel like I'm suddenly in *The Twilight Zone*," I groaned.

"Did he write that, too?" Virgil asked excitedly.

"No, and Dean Koontz didn't write *The Shining*."

"But your dad wrote *The Shining*, right?"

"No, Virgil. My dad is not Dean Koontz, nor is my dad Stephen King, who wrote *The Shining*."

"Huh," he said. "Well, that's what I tell people." The way he said this made me think that he didn't have any intention of changing this story in the future. He'd latched onto it as truth, and as far as he was concerned, whenever he discussed his sister-in-law, he would include the little bit about how my dad is Dean Koontz, the guy who wrote *The Shining*.

"These jalapeños would go great with a bloody Mary," Sandi said, opening the cabinet to get bloody Mary makings. "Amanda! Where's the booze?" she gasped. "And why am I seeing Honey Nut Cheerios instead of vodka?"

"Don't panic," I assured her. "I had to relocate the alcohol."

It only took me a few years to figure out that letting children play with liquor bottles is inappropriate. Our kitchen is small. There's only one suitable place to keep the booze, one shelf that will accommodate the tallest of liquor bottles. Unfortunately, this is also the shelf that is easiest accessed by toddlers. They never broke a bottle of booze or even attempted to open one, but they did like to rearrange them. At the age of two, Ivy would remove all of the bottles and carry them one by one over to her *Toy Story* table, where she would line them up over the background of Buzz and Woody's smiling faces. It was a game, a puzzle of sorts, and eventually she'd return them all to their shelf. She liked the pretty bottles, and with me standing there to ensure safety, I didn't have a problem with it. But on occasion, she would do this while wearing nothing but her diaper. This shouldn't matter, of course, but in my mind, her lack of clothing intensified the debauchery. I smiled at the sight of her but also felt an intense fear that a fire would spontaneously break out, causing the police and fire departments to rush into my home before I had a chance to tidy—because, of course, the few minutes I had before they arrived would be spent furiously applying makeup and searching for a more slimming outfit, as opposed to clothing my child or putting away the liquor bottles. They'd see Ivy in her diaper, presiding over rum, tequila, vodka, and perhaps an innocuous mixer like tonic, at which point they'd know that I am a very bad person.

Once this scenario played itself out in my head, I let Ivy play one last game of liquor store before moving the booze permanently out of reach. Other parents might think me slow or unfit for not curbing the behavior as soon as it started, but when it comes to positive parenting, I don't often get things right on the first or fourth try. I take baby steps.

"I had to move the liquor bottles out of reach from the kids," I told Sandi. "They're up there now." I pointed to a high cabinet, one that I realized was probably out of Sandi's reach as well.

"So lame," she said, staring wistfully at the cabinet.

"I don't have the goods, in any case," I said.

"That's all right. I just thought I'd swing by. I should probably head home and get some work done."

"Me, too," said Virgil. "I'm out."

"Those jalapeños really were *nummers*," Sandi said to Virgil as they headed for the door.

"Hey, did you hear about that dude that got caught with the thing in his car?"

"Yeah," she answered. "But at least he didn't kill a monkey."

* * *

CHAPTER TWO

Duct Tape for Dora

"Are you nervous?" Sandi asked.

This is the worst possible question someone can ask me. I'm instantly fearful that I've forgotten about an upcoming exam or that I have to teach a class on something about which I have no knowledge, like open heart surgery or rocket science. When I realize those scenarios are ridiculous and have no basis in reality, I wonder if I'm due to receive the results of a major biopsy. And if I've forgotten that today's the day the doctor tells me how long I'll live, then I must have Alzheimer's, even though I'm in my mid-thirties. At which point I decide to write my own obituary while I'm still lucid. I don't want anyone else screwing it up.

"Nervous about what?" I asked.

"About kindergarten."

"Why would I be nervous?" I crossed the obituary off my to-do list. "I'm not the one who has to learn to read."

"Yes, but are you nervous about sending Emilia to school?"

"Not at all," I said. "She's been in full-time daycare from the start. I think she'll be fine."

"But this is different. This is *kindergarten.*"

When Sandi tells me I should be nervous about something, I tend to believe her. She has two daughters with the same age difference as my girls, but her girls are older, so she experiences all the stages of parenthood a few years before I do. The way she said *kindergarten* made my heart tighten in my chest. Were there kindergarten hazing rituals that I didn't know about? Was there some sort of women's self-defense class for five-year-olds that I should enroll her in?

"I don't think Emilia's going to have any problems," I said.

"I agree. Emilia will be just fine. *You* might be a mess, though."

"We'll see."

I put my own emotional well-being to the side and gave some thought to how Emilia would do. Maybe *hazing* wasn't necessarily a worry, but would she be bullied or teased? Such scenarios are far more terrifying than physical playground injuries. Aside from the universal parental fear that another child might be mean to my own, and that I might inappropriately exact revenge on that child's mother by engaging in a cat fight at a PTA meeting, I held one other apprehension about the transition to kindergarten: nap time.

Emilia is a sleeper. Leading up to the first day of kindergarten, I tried to eradicate the nap in preparation and asked her daycare teachers for their assistance.

"We tried to keep her up," they'd report at the end of the day, "but she fell asleep anyway, right in the middle of painting." This would be evidenced by a large patch of blue paint in the middle of her forehead. The kid needs sleep. Even at the age of five, she enjoyed a two-hour nap during the day, despite the fact that she slept ten hours every night.

I shouldn't complain about this, as most parents equate the outgrowth of nap time to the death of a loved one. Nap time is a dear friend, that treasured hour or two when parents of small children regain some semblance of sanity. It's a time for parents to nap themselves, put away the dishes, or meet up for a nooner. Most of all, it's a time to steel oneself for the next segment of parenthood that extends from post-nap to bedtime.

Being the accommodating and gracious child that she is, Emilia continued to nap long after others her age stopped. This was a nice balance to Ivy, who cruelly refused to sleep through the night for three torturous years. Before she started kindergarten, we resigned ourselves to the possibilities that Emilia would either be very tired at the end of the day or fall asleep in the middle of class. Both would prove true.

I had no worries about Emilia's ability to handle actual schoolwork, and the introduction of homework into our daily routine excited me. That might sound insane, but when I was in school, I was a nerd and loved homework. I suspected that Emilia would too. And as far as Mike and I were concerned, homework meant less television, a break from which was welcome. Specifically, we longed for a hiatus from Dora and Diego, not simply because these animated little cousins insist on yelling everything that comes out of their mouths, but also because Dora and Diego had completely failed in teaching our children Spanish. They now think that maps can talk and believe monkeys wear boots, but their Spanish skills are still as limited as my own. I'd been hoping to cultivate little translators, but no such luck.

My mother, known to my children as Grammy, could not understand why I don't like Diego.

"But he's so cool," she said.

"No he's not. He's obnoxious. He's constantly yelling. Everything has to be at shouting volume, and the animation sucks."

"But he's an animal *rescuer*," she said. "He *rescues animals*." Grammy is an animal lover, and nothing is more appealing to her than the idea of someone who spends his life rescuing animals. Even if that someone is imaginary. "Speaking of animals," she continued, "maybe when they catch the monkey killer and put him on trial, I can fly out, and we can go to the trial together."

"Do they let people do that?" I asked.

"Why not?"

"Well, it's not like going to a concert or an exhibit at a museum."

"And we could take *snacks*," she continued.

"You want to see this guy hang, don't you?"

"He killed a monkey," she answered, which was her way of saying, *You bet your ass, I do.* "And maybe we could take Emilia and Ivy!"

"To a monkey murder trial?"

"They could learn about the justice system."

Grammy's idea was starting to sound like a good one, which was a reminder to myself that I should never be allowed to homeschool my children.

I abandoned this idea, as well as the fantasy of a cartoon making our children bilingual, and enrolled Emilia in a kindergarten class. Not just any kindergarten class. Half the day was taught in Mandarin Chinese. When Mike first brought this program's existence to my attention, I thought it sounded too intense and was worried about the stress it might cause Emilia.

"Are you excited about going to kindergarten?" I asked her.

"Will there be friends there who are this tall?" she countered, placing a flat palm on the top of her head.

"Yes, there will be plenty of other kids who are your age. And your height."

"Then yes, I'm excited."

"And you're going to learn Chinese there," I said.

"Okay. And will they have lunch there?"

"Yes," I assured her. "I promise you will continue to be fed on a regular basis."

If you think about it, telling a child she's going to learn Chinese is no more intimidating than showing her the face of a clock and telling her she's going to learn how to tell time. So Emilia's language exposure went from watching red-eyed tree frogs cry for *ayudame!* to hours of complex Chinese characters.

The elementary school we enrolled Emilia in, by way of lottery and wait-list, a process that reminded me of applying for college, was on the other side of town. Our daughter would spend the first half of the day in English with Ms. Sherod, and in the afternoon, she'd battle fatigue while learning to count in Chinese with Mr. Li. Both Ms. Sherod and Mr. Li are shockingly short, which is fitting for kindergarten teachers, as five-year-olds are low to the ground themselves. Both have an unmistakable knack for dealing with children, but also a firmness that makes it clear who is in charge. The confidence that I felt in Emilia's teachers made driving across town worth it.

I'll also take on a commute so that my children are not subjected to the incompetence of our local crossing guard. An old man sits in a plastic chair at an intersection near my house. When children approach, he is invariably sleeping, his chin resting heavy on his chest, or he's staring off into space. Conversely, when there are no children in sight, he can be found standing in the middle of the intersection, stop sign hanging down by his side, oblivious to the fact that the kids have long since made their way across the street safely, regardless of his ineptitude. I don't have any prejudices against the elderly, but if you reach the age when your faculties are diminished in any way, perhaps it's best not to assume a position in which you are responsible for the safety of children at a busy intersection.

As kindergarten approached, Sandi declared that she and her daughters would take Emilia shopping for a new backpack and lunchbox. This shopping event was touted for months and greatly anticipated. The day arrived, and Sandi, along with Emilia's beloved cousins, Bella and Rosie, took Emilia shopping. They returned all smiles and hopped up on sugar, Emilia lugging along a pink Barbie princess lunchbox as well as a pink plaid backpack. The amount of pink was to be expected. The size of the backpack was not.

"Wow, Emilia. Your new backpack is really... big," I said.

"That's the one she wanted," Sandi said by way of apology.

The backpack was more than half the size of my five-year-old and appeared to be in danger of weighing her down when empty. I imagined that filling it with a mere pencil and sheet of paper would cause her to topple over entirely. She inherited my sense of grace and therefore doesn't require much assistance when it comes to falling down.

"I love my pack-pack," Emilia declared, and the matter was put to rest.

When the long-awaited first day of kindergarten arrived, she spent the morning in tears, fretting over the backpack, which she now realized was far too big for her tiny frame. We cast it aside in favor of one of the five thousand pink Barbie princess backpacks we already had. I put aside the pink plaid monstrosity, which will come in handy if we are ever homeless and need to fit all of our belongings into a single bag.

I drove Emilia to school on the first day and walked her to the playground. Being the tyrant that I am, I insisted that she wear her coat in the freezing temperature, even though it covered the pink dress she'd been hoping to show off. When the bell rang, Ms. Sherod emerged.

"Line up, kids," she commanded. The children dutifully did so. "Now say goodbye to Mom and Dad," she instructed, and then led them into her class where the adults were not permitted. Mothers and fathers stood with expressions of abandonment, shocked that at that moment, our children didn't actually *need* us. When all of the children had made it inside, Ms. Sherod popped her head back out and said, "Believe me, it's better this way."

As I walked back to my car with a tingle in my throat, my heart felt light and fluttery. I attributed this not to the emotion of the experience, but to my heart condition that would surely cause me to drop dead on the spot. Then I remembered that I don't suffer from a heart condition so much as hypochondria, which meant that I wasn't going to drop dead, nor should I rush to the hospital to spend another two thousand dollars finding out that I still suffer from nothing worse than hypochondria.

I have no complaints with Emilia's school or teachers, except for one thing: they periodically lose my child or leave her unattended. Maybe I'm over-parenting, but I prefer that the responsible adults not misplace my daughter. On one occasion, it was because Emilia was sad about not completing an assignment, so she hid underneath a table at the end of the day while the other children exited. At least she broke the rules because she wanted to do more work, not because she was trying to get out of it. There have been a handful of instances where students played on the playground in the morning with no supervision. Whoever was scheduled to be on duty simply wasn't there, hopefully due to sudden kidney failure or alien abduction, because there really is no other valid excuse. The unsupervised playground was disconcerting, especially when you spend as much time as I do fretting about all of the sickos and whack jobs in the world.

One day I went to the school to retrieve Emilia, following her participation in an after-school program. I arrived seven minutes late. This is a parental sin, of course, but I'm only late for my children once every millennium, and this happened to be the day. I was rehearsing my apology and offer of monetary compensation to whichever adult was left waiting with her, when I pulled up to the school to see it deserted, except for my little girl waiting by herself, shivering and clutching the coat she refused to wear. She had a hopeful look on her face that could easily have turned to panic. I parked my car and walked to her. When she saw me, her eyes grew wide. She smiled big in joy and relief and ran to me.

"Mom!" she screamed. "I knew you'd come!"

"Of course." I hugged her. "I'll *always* come for you. But where's your teacher?"

"Um…" She looked around. "They left."

I hid from Emilia my disgust with myself for being late, along with my fury at the staff for leaving her alone. A volunteer had been assigned to wait with the children, and while I'm sure Emilia just slipped under the radar as opposed to being the target of willful neglect, there really are no excuses for such situations, not even aliens. Whenever I bring these matters to the attention of the school staff, they are incredibly apologetic and assure me that these mistakes won't happen again. Every single time.

In an effort to satisfy my curiosity regarding what goes on *inside* the classroom, I volunteered during the regular kindergarten portion of Emilia's day, as well as during the Chinese class. Volunteering never fails to renew my appreciation for teachers. Anyone who complains that teachers have it easy because they get their summers off needs to spend two hours (that's all it takes) volunteering in a kindergarten classroom. Suddenly you realize what teachers are up against. Personally, I would rather be a prison guard.

Volunteering in Mr. Li's class involved giving the children general guidance and keeping them in line. He'd just had a big talk with the class about how students are there to learn and not allowed to go to the bathroom every five minutes or keep getting up for a drink of water. Then a kid asked me if he could get a drink of water. Instinct always tells me to say yes when a child asks for water. I'd feel the same way if a child asked for a little more air to breathe. When my own children ask for water, I tell them they can have as much water as they want. As soon as I said yes, the boy shot up from his seat and ran to the water fountain. Mr. Li caught the movement out of the corner of his eye and stopped the boy, reminding him that only moments before he'd told them not to ask for any more drinks of water—each of them had already had a turn. The boy instantly turned and pointed to me with an outstretched arm and finger.

"Oh," I said sheepishly to the kindergarten teacher. "Yeah, that's my fault. I told him he could get a drink."

Mr. Li looked at me, obviously contemplating the value of having me assist in his classroom, and for a moment I thought I might be sent home.

Nonetheless, I enjoyed volunteering in both the morning and afternoon classes. I learned to count in Chinese, and the environment is one where compulsive use of hand sanitizer is praised instead of viewed as indicative of a personality disorder.

Emilia adjusted well to kindergarten, just as Mike and I made the decision to uproot our family and move to Mexico for the winter. Emilia would have three months of Chinese, followed by three months in Mexico before returning to Chinese class. I anticipated that this would leave her either extremely confused or a linguistic genius.

We'd made enough trips to Todos Santos, Mexico, where Mike's parents live, to figure out how to stay inexpensively and continue to work from there. The difficulty is not necessarily in going to Mexico, but in extracting oneself from the

States. It was time to have "the talk" with Emilia's teachers. Surely they'd judge me as irresponsible and naturally assume that I was putting my children in harm's way solely for the opportunity to get a tan and drink beer on the beach.

"Ms. Sherod?" I approached her at the end of the school day.

"Yes?"

"So… Uh…" *Wow*, I thought. *I am an absolute pussy.* My heart raced. "We're planning on leaving for a few months to go live in Mexico. Three. We're leaving for three months, but I'll do *whatever* I have to do to make sure Emilia keeps up with the rest of the class. Is that okay?" I can't pinpoint exactly what I was afraid of. It had been such a process to get Emilia into the school; maybe I feared that this trip could result in her being booted permanently. What if this resulted in Idaho school systems blackballing my children from their institutions and thereby forcing me to homeschool my children? I'd have to see if there were any juicy trials coming up. But Ms. Sherod smiled.

"If you have the opportunity to do something like that, you do it," she instructed. She leaned close and whispered in confidence, "It's just kindergarten." She was right. What a child learns from living in another country is far greater than any kindergarten curriculum. And Emilia would be enrolled in school while we were in Mexico. It's not as if she'd be watching television all day and eating tacos. But an even greater fear remained when I thought of telling Mr. Li. How on earth was I to keep up with the Chinese curriculum? I have many skills, but fluency in Mandarin Chinese is not one of them. Also, Mr. Li scared me just a little. This was not your typical smiles-and-rainbows kindergarten teacher. He was a no-nonsense task master. Children didn't fool around in Mr. Li's class. Children didn't get a second drink of water. And no one wants to be reprimanded, but being reprimanded in Chinese sounds especially harsh. Actually, even being praised in Chinese sounds harsh. But I told Mr. Li, and he, too, saw the big picture. Both teachers presented me with a wealth of materials to take with us to Mexico and asked that I just do my best in terms of keeping up from afar.

Neither Emilia nor Ivy had any objections about going to Mexico, either.

"Do they have chocolate in Mexico?" Ivy asked.

"Yes," I promised.

"Do they have friends that are this tall?" Emilia placed her hand on top of her head.

"Yes, you'll go to school there, and there will be kids your age. And your height."

"Do they have lunch in Mexico?" she asked.

"Every day."

* * *

CHAPTER THREE

The Burn Unit

"Mom, can we go *there* for lunch?" Emilia pointed to a strip mall, home of China Grand Buffet.

"No."

"But look, that's Chinese, just like at my school." She indicated the characters next to the words China Grand Buffet. Utilizing my degree in linguistics, I deduced that these characters meant: China Grand Buffet.

"I promise someday I will take you to a Chinese restaurant, but it won't be China Grand Buffet."

"Why not?"

"It's a family rule," I explained. "We don't eat at buffets."

Personally, I think buffets are disgusting and bear some responsibility in terms of what's wrong with this country. Whenever I find myself in a political conversation regarding Things That Are Wrong With This Country, I always offer up my opinion of buffets. I'm typically then shunned from further conversation, which reverts back to questions of church and state and gun rights and international policy and partisan politics. But think about it. Buffets are wrong on many levels. No one should actually *eat all they can eat.* This thinking is fundamentally wrong. An attempt to consume all that is physically possible for your body to consume is the epitome of gluttony. And the thinking that this is economical is severely flawed. The idea that you should overeat to get your money's worth makes no sense. It's not as if you can eat the next day's meals, thereby stocking up on your body's food requirements. The body can only take so much food at a time, and you're going to need to eat again later anyway, so stuffing yourself is just gross. I flatly forbid anyone in my immediate family from frequenting the buffets in our town, including any place with a name along the lines of Chuck-A-Rama. What does that even mean? Is Chuck the proprietor of this establishment, or does "Chuck" relate to "upchuck"? While healthier, more unique eating establishments have had to close their doors, Chuck-A-Rama is going strong, at least in Idaho. What's wrong with this country? Buffets.

Emilia accepted my refusal to go to China Grand Buffet, and when we arrived home, I decided to reward both girls with a healthier endeavor, but one that would still be considered a treat: I broke out the Slip 'n Slide. What I'd forgotten was that my children are too timid to enjoy use of the Slip 'n Slide unless they have older kids like their cousins to show them how it's done. It took me about forty-five minutes of wrestling with various hoses to set up the Slip 'n Slide, followed by another twenty minutes assessing and poorly remedying the leaks, so I was determined that they were going to have fun on the fucking wet piece of plastic, even if they broke their necks in the process.

"Just run and slide, run and slide," I coached them, but without someone to go before them, they refused.

"I don't want to," said Emilia.

"I'm scared," said Ivy.

"Come on, kids, this is super fun!" I cheered.

They held each other's hands in solidarity and took a defiant step back from the Slip 'n Slide.

"Fine," I said. "Wait here." I went inside and put on my bathing suit, which is a bikini I've had longer than my children. Deftly avoiding all mirrors in the house, I made my way back outside and demonstrated the run and slide technique. Maybe I've lost my inner child or forgotten what fun feels like, but I'm sad to report that using a Slip 'n Slide as an adult results in absolutely zero enjoyment. Especially when one is self-conscious about wearing a bikini that's three sizes too small. Bumping my way along the yellow plastic was an excellent way to highlight the jiggling of my belly. In addition, the Slip 'n Slide was in our front yard, and I wasn't enjoying the thought of any of the neighbors witnessing the aforementioned jiggling, followed by the pathetic lumbering of my body as I attempted to get up off the ground, cold, wet, chubby, and covered with unwanted souvenirs of nature.

Our backyard is enormous, the sort of backyard better suited to *Brady Bunch* families with oodles of kids, or people who like to keep dogs and chickens and goats, or someone who needs ample room with which to dispose of an occasional body. It is fenced on all sides and may very well have been used as the backdrop for a Slip 'n Slide commercial at some point in history. There is no reasonable explanation for why I would have set up the Slip 'n Slide in the *front* yard. Maybe

I'd thought the neighbors would see my kids in the midst of gleeful summer fun and we'd instantly be endeared to them, at which point they'd decide to bake us cookies. But once I became a swimsuit-wearing participant, this plan backfired. We abandoned the Slip 'n Slide and went back inside. I forgot to avoid the mirrors this time.

Seeing myself in a bikini was distressing, especially in light of the fact that in just a few months we would travel to Mexico, where I would have frequent occasions to wear a bathing suit. I'd managed on a previous trip to avoid doing so, but avoiding wearing a bathing suit in Mexico is just as depressing as not looking good in a bathing suit, because the fact that you're not in one is a constant reminder of exactly *why* you are not in one. And even though I can get around it because I don't particularly like to swim or frolic in the surf, you can't drink as much beer at the beach as I do and eventually not have to visit the ocean for a quick pee.

I changed focus and tried on some of my old sundresses to see if they still fit. They did not, which I realized long before I got them on, because sadly, I could not get them on. I thought I might suffocate at one point when I managed to get a sundress over my head, and it began strangling my neck and arms, unable to progress any further down my body. I can't blame the sundresses, and I realized that they were at least ten years old. They literally had dust on them. If I haven't worn clothing in so long that it's gathered dust, chances are it's not going to fit. A decade is not kind to the body. A decade including two pregnancies is downright brutal. I momentarily deluded myself into thinking that I didn't *want* to wear the sundresses because after ten years, they were no doubt out of style. This is laughable, as nothing I wear is ever necessarily in style, and I faced facts that it had nothing to do with fashion and everything to do with the size of my body.

I told myself it was time to get serious, which I'd said on many prior occasions, but this time I really meant it. Sandi taught a Piyo class in town, so I thought I'd give it a try. I love yoga, and Piyo comes from the words *Pilates* and *yoga;* I thought it would be a good fit. The class took place in the upstairs room of a gymnastics studio. When I showed up, I noticed that I was by far the youngest person in the class. *I got this*, I told myself. But this wasn't the first time I'd given myself too much credit for being younger. Fifteen minutes into the class, I knew I was in trouble. Sure, there were some yoga poses, but they were performed at hyper speed. One segment of the class seemed entirely devoted to figuring out how to make pushups even more difficult than they already are. Is that really necessary? Pushups are plenty hard as it is. Even *girl* pushups are hard. Someone making you do pushups while keeping one leg off the ground or extended out to the side is both cruel and unusual, and I silently cursed my sister-in-law for being that someone. When the class got really tough, I looked at the unforgiving wall of mirrors before me and realized that while I might be younger than everyone else, I was also fatter. I made it through two classes (barely) before conveniently being busy during all future class times.

At the same time as my Piyo failures, I discovered Pinterest. If you have not yet ventured into the world of Pinterest, I can tell you that the purpose of this site is to share recipes for disgustingly fattening foods, most of which fall into the meat-plus-cheese casserole category (the type that would nicely complement a Chuck-A-Rama buffet), and to share various exercises, which one must undertake in earnest to reverse the effects of the aforementioned casseroles. I have one Pinterest friend who displays a frightening obsession with Marilyn Monroe. Thus, when I visit Pinterest, I am assaulted by a variety of half-naked Marilyn pictures, psycho-killer ab exercises, and directions on how to make deep-fried cheddar beer pork balls in lard gravy.

Luckily, we had an impending houseguest, one who had dietary restrictions that thwarted any aspirations I might have had of preparing the aforementioned pork balls. Kelly is one of Mike's college buddies and handy to have around, the sort of guy who can construct a working vehicle out of random items from your junk drawer. Of course, with all this knowledge and innate ability comes a ridiculous appreciation for things like *Star Wars* and discussions of electromagnetic fields and solar power and who would win in a battle between Godzilla and the Predator. These aren't things that I often think about or dwell on, so sometimes when Kelly speaks of these things, my eyes glaze over. He abruptly stops speaking and asks, "Amanda? Did I lose you again?" Sometimes a conversation with Kelly will involve how cool it is that a certain device has so much RAM or so many gigs or such and such bandwidth. I nod and smile with only a vague notion of what sort of device we're even talking about. Perhaps it slow cooks pork balls or harnesses nuclear energy. I stop him mid-sentence.

"I'm sorry, Kelly, but I just don't speak this language." Then he'll continue, trying to explain it to me in words I understand, dumbing the concept down so that someone on my non-techie level can comprehend. I interrupt him after another five minutes and say, "I'm sorry, Kelly. Now I kind of understand, but I still don't care."

* * *

Kelly's biggest struggle in life is with food, which is why his visit put the kibosh on pork balls; I just wouldn't do that to him. He's tried numerous combinations of diet and exercise, all to no avail until he discovered HCG. This is popular for weight loss, but also a chemical that the body produces during pregnancy, which goes against all logic, because the only weight loss associated with pregnancy is when you actually give birth or when you throw up from the nausea. And personally, I'm disinclined to try anything that I have to obtain from another country or that requires I give myself injections, which is how Kelly takes his HCG. Equally troubling is the idea that the body is supposed to survive on five hundred calories per day when using HCG.

"I need to find a really big apple," Kelly once said.

"Why?"

"Because today I'm allowed to have an apple."

"You're six feet tall, Kelly. Perhaps you should eat more than an apple."

"Don't worry," he said. "I'm also allowed one ounce of chicken with no seasoning."

Kelly talks a lot. In fact, Kelly talks constantly, so when he approached me in the kitchen one day but seemed at a loss for words, I knew something was up.

"So, Amanda, I... I was going to ask you... What would you think..."

"Spit it out, Kelly. What's up?"

"I don't know how to say this…"

"That's ridiculous, Kelly. You talk more than anyone else I know."

"I have some extra HCG if you want to try it."

The difficult thing for Kelly to voice wasn't that he was trying to be my drug dealer; by offering me HCG, he was admitting that I *needed* HCG. In essence, he gave voice to the fact that I *was* chubby. As a male, he was well aware of how dangerous such an action could be. There is an unspoken rule that men must never admit that a woman is fat, despite the fact that the evidence might be literally overwhelming. If a woman sits on a chair only to have it break apart underneath her massive form, a man is supposed to help her to her feet and immediately begin criticizing the poor craftsmanship of what was once a perfectly fine chair. Women don't get fatter; our clothes get smaller. And one should never inquire about a due date until a woman explicitly says, "I am pregnant, and there is a baby growing inside me." We all know these rules. Kelly braced in the event that my head would spin around or in case I attempted to remove his heart from his chest with my bare hands. To his obvious relief, I responded with a mere, "No thanks."

During certain phases of Kelly's HCG diet, he's permitted to eat a specific kind of sugar-free pudding. This is the closest Kelly now allows himself to get to the sugar binges of his former life. The times when he's allowed pudding coincide with when he's also permitted to drink alcohol. When Kelly is drunk, he approaches pudding not with a spoon, but as a lover reunited with his greatest desire after a prolonged absence. He literally crushes the pudding cup against his face. The easiest way to tell if Kelly is suffering from a hangover is not from the typical clues of bloodshot eyes or a general air of queasiness, but whether or not he has a ring of dried chocolate pudding circling his mouth. There are times when I think we might need to consider a pudding intervention. As someone with enough addictions of my own, I don't need to add pudding into the mix, so this was yet another reason for me to pass on his offer of HCG.

Most women who struggle with their weight as I do hate to have their picture taken. It wouldn't be so bad if there was physically a means of sucking in one's neck, but as yet, I haven't figured out how to do this. I've heard women talk about how they wish they could Photoshop their face onto the body of someone thinner. I would take the opposite approach. I'd rather have my face Photoshopped onto the body of someone who is much larger. That way, when people saw me in the flesh, they'd think I look fantastic. Having a really flattering picture of yourself just prepares the world to be disappointed with the real you.

Though I worry about my weight, I try to avoid a lot of the other stupid worries that females have and the corresponding rituals that women put themselves through. Not all though. Every other month, I have my hair colored. And every six weeks, I get my hoo-hoo waxed. I'd like to keep it at that. I don't need my nails painted or eyebrows threaded or lashes extended. I want to simplify, not add on. The human body requires a ridiculous amount of maintenance as it is. I see no need to add one more thing to my to-do list so that my eyelashes can look freakishly long. And as far as eyebrows, I don't know what threading them means, but I hear it's incredibly painful.

Waxing the nether regions is ridiculous and painful and expensive and unnecessary. I recognize this and once suggested to my husband that I should give it up, during a discussion of what luxuries we could forgo to get our finances in order. Mike responded with an immediate and emphatic *no*, both to the idea of giving up waxing as well as ceasing to pay someone to mow the lawn. Apparently he feels that landscaping of any kind, be it upon lawn or bush, is money well spent. So I'll continue to do it for him, even though it involves assuming the most vulnerable position one can possibly assume. If you think about it, paying someone to painfully rip the hair off your asshole is about as stupid a thing as I can think of. And the fact that the client and aesthetician can carry on a mundane conversation about weather and celebrities and what to get the kids this year for Christmas while one person places hot wax on the other's vagina is ridiculous. This is the epitome of the stupid female ritual.

Another moronic thing women put themselves through is burning one's face off. I know it has a technical name like chemical peel, but really it's burning one's face off. I stopped in at my husband's office one day, where Sandi also works. She was wearing a huge hat pulled down low over her face. When she looked up, my first instinct was to call 9-1-1.

"Jesus, Sandi, what the hell happened to you?"

"One of my clients gave me a free chemical peel. I know it looks bad now, but when it all heals, my skin is going to look incredible!" She tried to smile then, but stopped when her face began to crack.

"Does that hurt?"

"Yes, this is unbelievably painful. But it was free."

"Well, I'm glad you didn't pay someone to do that to you."

The irony of making yourself hideous so that you can look pretty is startling, but we do it all the time.

At one point, we actually sent her home from the office because she looked too frightening to be on display to the general public.

"Sandi," Mike said, "I think you should go home."

"I can't. I'm meeting with clients."

"You don't understand. You *can't* meet clients."

"Is it really that bad?"

"Yes, children are scared of you. You look like a burn victim."

"Well, technically I *am* a burn victim."

"I'm going to have to call bullshit on that," I interjected. "If you willingly subject yourself to something like that, and you do so in the name of vanity, you don't get to put yourself in league with someone who was trapped in a burning house or had acid thrown in her face. You're not a victim; you're a willing participant."

"Did I mention it was free?"

* * *

CHAPTER FOUR

What Rhymes With Porn?

Four weeks later, Sandi's face was almost healed, though it was now discolored in patches. The end result of her chemical peel was that it left her skin blotchier than it had been at the start. But, as Sandi continued to remind us, "At least it was free!" As if this somehow makes the pain and horror and facial discoloration all worthwhile. At least it was free pain, free horror, and free facial discoloration. When she finally stopped looking like something had gnawed her face off, my mother-in-law and father-in-law, known in our house as Nana and Papa, arrived for a visit. Papa had been given a chemical of his own to apply to his head and face. This was not in the interests of vanity, but to eradicate any potentially cancerous spots from his skin. The result of this treatment, however, was two weeks of looking like something had gnawed *his* face off. Nana was concerned about how the children would react and had called us before their arrival.

"His face looks really bad. I just want to warn you because I don't want the kids to be scared."

"Don't worry," I assured her. "They survived seeing their Aunt Sandi, and that was pretty bad."

I *was* worried though. Not about my children being scared, but about them reacting negatively to their Papa and thereby hurting his feelings. He's an adult, of course, but there's a noticeable sting when a child is repulsed by you, no matter your age. I'll never forget the dinner party during which I interrupted my hostess duties to answer a question for Emilia. After I did so, she loudly proclaimed, "Mom, your breath is *really* stinky. Ew!" She said this while furiously waving her hand in front of her nose, as if I'd shat myself in the crowded room. Since I don't beat her, there wasn't much recourse at the time but to shoot daggers at her with my eyes, laugh it off with a hand over my mouth, and then disappear to brush my teeth and gargle.

When Papa did show up, I was relieved to see that his treatment wasn't even close to the level of horror Sandi experienced. I still held my breath when Emilia gasped at the first sight of her maligned Papa.

"Wow!" she said. "Papa, I love your pretty red face!"

While the in-laws were visiting, Boise held its annual Balloon Classic. This is a three-day event of hot air balloons and related activities. On the evening of the last night, they line up all the hot air balloons on the ground and then inflate them so that they glow in the night. I'd heard about this but never seen it firsthand. When I mentioned it to the rest of the group, both my father-in-law and husband offered little more than a bored-sounding "hmm." You'd have thought they regularly saw a dozen hot air balloons glowing in the night. But this is one of those things that I've learned to let slide; there's little point in trying to engender excitement in someone who just doesn't care. I was reminded of my reaction to Kelly when he tried to get me to watch *Battlestar Galactica*.

There was no way the children would be able to stay awake and conduct themselves with acceptable behavior past nine o'clock, so taking them was out of the question. My mother-in-law, on the other hand, was available and as excited about the event as I was. We decided we'd go check it out, just the two of us. After a ten-minute drive, we parked a few blocks from the event and walked the rest of the way, preferring the walk to the anxiety we'd experience vying for a parking space with thousands of other people. I feel that 90 percent of the population loses all logic and decency when entering a parking lot, suddenly behaving as if we're living out the *Hunger Games*. I have taken a sacred vow never to become one of those people, with the exception of when I am old and feeble, at which time I will park wherever I damn well please, and I will assault any officer who attempts to give me a ticket with my tennis-ball-tipped walker.

"Wow, this is amazing!" Nana said as we approached the hot air balloons.

"Yes," I agreed. "It's beautiful."

"Yes, this is really something."

"Quite a treat. Not something you see every day."

"Would you ever want to go up in one?" she asked.

"Oh *hell* no."

"Me neither," she agreed. "Let me buy you a beer."

"That's a great idea." I looked around at the various vendors. "I don't know where the beer tent is."

"Let's try this way," she suggested. We randomly set off

in one direction and passed by people selling pizza and corn dogs and cookies and lemonade, but no beer.

"Let's try the other way," I said, but we found more of the same.

"This is crazy. I can't believe they're not selling beer here."

"That can't be. It would be both cruel and ridiculous."

"Amanda, look," she whispered, discreetly pointing to a couple seated on a picnic blanket, each with a beer in hand.

"Excuse me," I interrupted them, "but where did you get that?" For a second, I contemplated pretending to be the Beer Police and demanding that she hand over all of her alcohol to me if she wanted to avoid a citation.

I motioned to the woman's beer, and she gave me a smile edged in pity. She wouldn't have been fooled by the Beer Police ruse. "We brought it from home."

"Oh." I leaned in wistfully, and she eased back, just as her husband nonchalantly sat on their cooler. It appeared thievery was out of the question.

Eventually, regretfully, Nana and I resigned ourselves to the fact that there was no beer at this particular festival— unless you brought it with you. Perhaps this was for the safety of everyone involved, considering the amount of propane and flame present. In any case, there wasn't any beer. I wouldn't do anything so rash as to boycott this type of event in the future, but you can be damned sure that I'll have a flask or cooler or both at next year's festival. Beer is as important at outdoor events in the summer as sunscreen, water, and Porta Potties, and its absence seemed like a crime against nature herself.

* * *

The following night, I prepped dinner, and Papa hung around the kitchen to keep me company. "How's Mike doing?" he asked. "Have you gotten the results of his autopsy yet?"

"His *what?*"

"His autopsy."

"Well, I hope not. Last I checked, he's still very much alive."

"Who's still very much alive?" Mike asked, walking into the kitchen.

"You are," I answered. "Your dad just asked if we'd gotten the results of your autopsy yet."

"Wait," Papa demanded, "that's not what I meant." He clenched his eyes shut tight in frustration, searching for the right word. "You're going to write about this, aren't you?"

"No, I promise."

"His *biopsy.*" He turned to Mike. "Did you get the results of your biopsy?"

Our family provides near-constant business for a local dermatologist. We are a steady string of skin cancer scares. I'm the only one that sees the bright side of this; every time the dermatologist removes a chunk of flesh, I've just achieved some small measure of weight loss.

"I'm fine," Mike said. "I just have to keep a close eye on the spots they removed."

"Oh, well that's good."

"Amanda?" Nana called from the living room.

"Yes?"

"I'm in a bit of a quandary over whether I should buy a laptop or a tabletop. Do you have any thoughts on that?" For a second, I thought maybe she was deciding whether to buy a computer or a table on which she could write with old-fashioned pen and paper. But then I remembered that these were my in-laws, for whom communication is often a challenge, as just evidenced by my father-in-law's inquiry regarding his son's autopsy.

"You mean a laptop or a *desk*top?"

"Yes, a laptop or a tabletop. Which do you think I should buy?"

"A laptop," I answered.

"But wouldn't a tabletop be cheaper?"

"Unless you're looking at a big slab of marble or granite, yes, a tabletop would probably be cheaper than a laptop."

Virgil entered with a booming "Shaka-kahn," and I left Nana to figure out on her own whether she wanted to purchase a computer or a hunk of Formica.

"Hi, Uncle Virgil!" the girls greeted him.

"Ivy," he said. "I heard you're wearing underpants like a big girl. Is that true?"

"Yes," Ivy beamed, recently having made the leap out of diapers.

"Good, because I don't like diapers. I'll never forget when my cousin Matthew was a baby, and he was walking along with this huge, saggy diaper, and it was like dragging on the ground, and this piece of—"

"Virgil!" I interrupted.

At this point, Ivy spotted a nearby Barbie and lost interest in the conversation. This particular Barbie was clothed. Whenever Ivy locates a clothed Barbie, she is immediately compelled to make Barbie naked. This behavior might concern me had I not been in a dozen other households also brimming with naked Barbies.

Virgil turned to me and continued. "What? I wasn't going to say shit. I was going to say poop. Would you give me some credit? So anyway, Matthew's walking along, and this little round ball, I mean like a perfect little brown sphere of shit pops out of his diaper. How does that even happen? So I pick it up and smell it."

Having overheard, Mike said, "Only you would smell something that fell out of a diaper."

"You just never know when it comes to poop," said Virgil.

"Nothing you say makes any sense," I said.

"Sure it does. I smell shit all the time. I *always* smell my socks."

"You're full of it."

"Oh, come on. Are you telling me you don't smell your socks? Don't you want to know if they smell like detergent or like foot fungus? That's the sort of info a man needs to know. Not smelling your socks is like practicing bad hygiene."

This is one of those things that Virgil says and initially you don't believe him, but eventually you find out that he does, in fact, smell his socks on a regular basis. Or maybe he starts smelling his socks to turn his fabrication into reality. The same can be said of his habit with Tabasco. He used to talk about how he'd use half a bottle of Tabasco on his dinner. We called bullshit on him, so he began literally dumping half a bottle of Tabasco on his dinner whenever he came to eat with us. As someone who prides herself on her cooking—and cooking with spice, at that—this was disconcerting. Equally disconcerting is eating next to someone who is sweating profusely and looks to be in danger of keeling over from a heart attack at the age of thirty-five. By this point though, he's all in. There's no turning back, so he continues on, waging a ridiculous battle with himself, his family, and a Tabasco-drenched plate of enchiladas.

"I would like to request that we not discuss diapers, poop, or socks while we eat," I said.

"Thank you," said Virgil. "I appreciate that because if there's one thing I can't stand, it's when this family has to go on and on about something that's gross, especially during dinner. It just gives me the willies."

"You're the one who brings this stuff up," said Mike.

"No, I don't. I talk about current events and shit. Like that snake that ate an alligator and exploded—did you see that? They have pictures of it online. It's fucking nasty. Can I use someone's computer? I have to check PlentyofFish.com."

"No," said Mike.

"Dinner's ready," I announced.

We sat down to a lovely meal, a typical Turner gathering that involved learning more than we ever wanted to know about Virgil's hygiene habits and the reasons he buys baby powder in bulk. At one point, Nana broke out into her customary family hymn of Sister Sledge, though she only knows one line, so she actually just sang "We are family" five times in a row before realizing that no one was going to join in. Mike and Virgil rolled their eyes at each other while Papa pretended not to hear. Though we feign discomfort with Nana's enthusiasm for family, we secretly admit that it's part of her charm and love her dearly for it.

* * *

The night after we have a houseful of family over for dinner, we often give the kitchen a rest and take the girls to Casanova's, our favorite pizza place. We entered, and Emilia announced to the room at large: "This is my favorite restaurant!" She did this unprompted, and I thought we deserved a free order of something fried for her enthusiasm.

We ordered the Caesar first, the only menu item I've found that results in my children willingly and gleefully devouring greens. Sure, those greens are drenched in Caesar salad dressing, but the greens and the good things they contain make their way into my kids' tiny bodies, and that makes me happy. The croutons (or "frootocks" as she calls them) are Ivy's favorite, but as long as she keeps eating the lettuce, I'm willing to throw a crouton on top. We waited for the pizza and played a few rounds of I Spy. When this ran its course, the girls practiced their rhyming skills.

Emilia: "House, mouse! That rhymes, Mama!"

Ivy: "Purple, wurple! That rhymes, Mama!"

They continued on in a volume much louder than necessary, ensuring that the entire restaurant was aware of their rhyming prowess, until we inevitably hit more colorful language.

"Pick, dick!"

"More, whore!"

Mike choked on crouton.

"Corn, porn!"

It was dumb luck that resulted in three profanities in a row. And I couldn't reprimand them, because they didn't know the meaning of what they said. If I did reprimand them, I'd essentially be pointing out bad language of which they were previously unaware.

"Let's use our *quiet* voices! Who wants more salad?" I asked as Mike regained composure and craned his neck toward the kitchen, hoping the pizza was en route so that we could use it as a gag with which to silence our children.

I thought about pulling a Nana and breaking out into song. If not Sister Sledge, maybe a little "YMCA" that the kids could participate in. But personally, I'd rather hear little children practice their rhyming with unintentionally colorful language than listen to their mom in a rendition of the Village People, and I figured my fellow patrons would feel the same.

* * *

CHAPTER FIVE

Are We There Yet?

When my kids are at school, I miss them terribly. I picture their smiling faces, their innocence and humor, and I can't wait to pick them up. After a few minutes in the car with them on the way home, I've had enough. It's distressing how quickly my mood changes, but one needs only thirty seconds of whining, complaining, and seat kicking to have their fill of chauffeuring.

Getting *in* the car is easier than it used to be. We no longer have ten minutes of tears over whether or not I've buckled the seatbelt of a child who really wanted to do it all by herself, or tantrums regarding which child got into the car first. Both children can now open their own doors, though for Ivy this involves grabbing the door handle with both hands and standing on the tire, then throwing her weight back, which is just barely enough to open the door. It's adorable and terrifying at the same time.

When we get in the car, Ivy speaks incessantly. It's almost as if, inside a moving vehicle, she is physically unable to stop talking.

"Mom, there's a bird. Mom, I'm going to be a tent for Halloween. Mom, I'm going to have chocolate chips and ice cream and candy for my birthday. Mom? Mom!"

"*What*, Ivy?" I try not to sound exasperated. I fail.

"I'm just kidding." She laughs before launching into the next monologue. "Mom, I love chocolate sprinkles and there's a bird flying and when I grow up I'm going to like coffee and when I grow up I will drink wine and I want to marry a girl, not a boy. Let's go to the aquarium and then let's go home and then let's have some chocolate sprinkles."

"Hey, Ivy. Let's see if we can stop talking for just a minute. Let's try it, okay?"

"Okay." This is followed by a blissful, if brief, moment of silence. If I wasn't driving at the time, I would close my eyes and revel in it.

"Mom, I'm not talking."

It's not that I detest riding in the car or that it's always negative. Occasionally the ride home from school results in wonderful conversations.

"Mom?" Emilia asked. "Why do our eyes cry sometimes when we're not sad?"

"Well, our eyes can tear for lots of different reasons. Sometimes they tear when we're happy or tired or feeling something special."

"Mom, sometimes when we say the Pledge of Legions, my eyes tear."

"That's okay," I said. "That just means you're feeling an emotion."

"Mom, remember when we went to the fire station?" The week prior, Emilia's class had gone to the local fire station for a field trip.

"Yes," I answered.

"Well, there was a fireman there, and he was really handsome."

I had no idea that my five-year-old knew the word *handsome*.

"Yes?"

"And when he talked to me, my eyes teared."

"Oh." I smiled. "That's okay."

"But I didn't love him, Mom. Only my *eyes* did."

"Okay, Emilia. Only your eyes loved him."

"Mom?" asked Ivy.

"Yes."

"Can we play Wacky Wednesday?"

"Sure, Ivy. You can go first."

"How about… a monkey was in a tree with chocolate sprinkles!"

"Wow, Ivy, that's really wacky!"

"My turn," said Emilia. "What if a giraffe had wings and was wearing a pink dress!"

"Oh, that's so silly," I said.

"Your turn, Mom," said Emilia.

"Okay, what if a house was made out of Jell-O!" Ivy dutifully laughed at this, but I could tell from Emilia's silence that she was going to challenge whether or not it was truly wacky.

"Mom, that's silly, but that's not how you play the game because remember in that movie there was a house made out of Jell-O, so that one doesn't count." The movie she spoke of was *Cloudy with a Chance of Meatballs*, and while I didn't think that should disqualify me, I couldn't entirely disagree with her that it wasn't the most original thing I could have come up with.

"Okay, I'll try again," I said.

"No, Mom. That was your turn. You have to wait for it to be your turn again."

"Oh."

"It's Ivy's turn."

"How about... a hippo was in a tree with chocolate sprinkles!"

I laughed because I knew that's what I was supposed to do, but I also knew that Emilia was now firmly wearing her Wacky Wednesday Police hat and that she was going to take issue with Ivy.

"Ivy, you said that last time."

"No, she didn't," I said. "Last time it was a monkey."

"Fine," Emilia huffed. It occurred to me that she felt much like I do when we try to play Candy Land and all I want in the world is for the two of them to follow the rules.

"Go ahead, Emilia," I said.

"Mom, what if you were as big as a house!"

"Yeah," Ivy chimed in. "What if you were really, *really* big, Mom?"

They seemed to really get a kick out of this idea, so much so that I almost blurted out "What if Mommy ran the car over a unicorn and it died!" just to get them on a different topic, even if it was one that involved tears.

Instead of emotionally scarring my children, I resolved once again to get serious about getting into shape. For real, this time. The fact that I was overly sensitive to the girls' use of my size when playing Wacky Wednesday was an indication that I either needed to do something about it or just stop worrying. I've never excelled at the cessation of worry, so I decided to take another stab at physical health while continuing to let my mental insecurities flourish.

I used to think of healthy people as those who don't engage in any sort of vice, as people who exercise and meditate and eat All-Bran and are blessed with a perfect sense of well-being and contentment with their place in the universe. This image of health immediately removed itself as a possibility for me, because while I have been known to literally run my ass off so that I can control outward expansion, I'm not willing to do so unless I can enjoy a beverage afterward. I know how to work hard, but only if it is accompanied by visions of a cocktail at the end of the day. But maybe my love of alcohol didn't have to preclude me from being healthy, because I began to notice a lot of "healthy" individuals who party in a manner reminiscent of *Animal House*. These are fitness buffs that stay active not to be healthy, but to counteract the regular damage they inflict upon themselves. They have to make huge strides in terms of diet and exercise in the daytime to counteract the debauchery they regularly engage in when the sun goes down. I feel a shameful satisfaction whenever I see a health nut get sloshed. It proves that while they may walk around with superior physiques, their sculpted bodies are just as vulnerable to booze as the rest of us lard asses. The right amount of vodka can level any playing field.

My in-laws are good examples of people who exercise enough to make even that perfectly bone-structured hottie doctor on afternoon television feel bloated and slothful. At the same time, they're known to party like rock stars five nights out of seven. They're retired physical education teachers, very active and healthy when not in rock-star mode, so you'd think that I'd get into shape when they're around, but the opposite is true. When Nana and Papa visit, happy hour gets earlier every day. My only saving grace is that I have to pick my children up around five o'clock. This keeps me from participating in the early-afternoon martini.

My motivation for getting in shape wasn't just because my in-laws were staying with us and I had to counteract the corresponding nightly overindulgence, but also because my in-laws are so maddeningly fit. It's hard not to want to improve your body when you realize that your sixty-five-year-old mother-in-law, who is a foot shorter than you and is constantly teaching Zumba and lifting weights, could easily kick your ass. My father-in-law is no slouch, either. Not content with riding his bike along the existing trails in the deserts of Baja, he takes along a machete and spends hours cutting new trails down steeper and more treacherous inclines.

With the constant flow of beverages during my in-laws' visit, I knew it was once again time to try a new form of exercise. In high school, I'd played soccer, so I looked up the local adult league. I was excited about joining the over-thirty team but then found that they were booked. So I joined a women's team that had no minimum age. The team was comprised of me at thirty-five and a dozen girls in their late teens and early twenties. They were happy to have me, as I play goalie, a position not everyone is willing to take.

Before my first game, we chatted on the sidelines. None of my teammates had children or muffin tops, and they texted with enough speed to create sparks, but I was sure that beyond that, we must have things in common. When the game began, I immediately noticed that a few of my teammates had exceptional footwork. I also noticed that those same players looked startlingly fierce, as if they were mustering up the meanest expressions their perfect little, wrinkle-free faces could produce. Doubtless they had spent hours practicing in a mirror, trying to look mean. Then I noticed the growling, grunting, and body checking. Had I signed up for rugby by mistake? This behavior came only from my team. My teammates were overly aggressive, antagonistic, and played with a swagger I'd sooner associate with the overinflated egos of male football players. One girl actually tried to start a fistfight with members of the other team. If I'd been in my teens or twenties, it would have been a perfect fit, a great outlet for the angry, youthful me who, for some reason, craved a bit of confrontation and bloodshed, but I'd grown up. I didn't engage in fistfights; I recycled packaging and looked both ways before crossing the street.

Our opponents, who were competitive but slightly more normal, were as shocked as I was by the behavior of my team of bullies, and I quickly deduced that they were also people who recycled packaging and looked both ways before crossing the street. They held their own, but I could see their frustration at having to play a bunch of assholes. Having my kids on the sidelines was as appropriate as planting them on the couch for a *CSI* marathon. Nonetheless, I played well, and we won the game, procuring a few yellow cards in the process.

Later that day, I could barely walk. I thought I might die and imagined the headlines: "Muffin-Top Mama Tries to Play Soccer: Dead After *First* Game." I'd been a runner for some time, so I didn't anticipate that I'd have any physical trouble playing a game of soccer once a week. But when I run, I do so at a nice gentle pace along a tree-lined path. I'm relaxed and carry hydration and electrolyte-replenishing products in my runner's version of a fanny pack. Soccer was a different animal, involving short bursts of energy and sprinting from side to side. My body was not accustomed to this type of movement and severely rebelled against it. Lord help me if I'd had to run the full length of the field instead of darting back and forth in front of the goal, which brought to mind another headline: "Sucky Soccer Mom Only Played *Goalie*." I figured I should just keep going though, that my body simply needed to adjust.

A week after the first game, at my second, I was still sore but committed to playing. After this game, during which my team once again displayed the worst possible sportsmanship and made me embarrassed to call myself a member, I again couldn't walk and again thought that I might die. "Wussy Mom Eats Shit on Field and Dies."

It took a few weeks to fully recover this time, and I didn't play again. I held little remorse about letting down my team because I'd come to associate soccer with mean girls, and I didn't want to be a part of them anyway. In hindsight, I spent about $200 on gear for a game that I played twice. I'd purchased used cleats, shin guards, a ball, goalie gloves, a goalie jersey, socks, and shorts. It's much easier to spend money on ideas than it is to see them through.

Putting soccer behind me, I looked around for another means of getting in shape. My body was too used to running at that point, and I needed something new. In the corner of our bedroom, gathering dust for almost a year, sat a kettle bell and set of DVDs I'd bought Mike the previous Christmas. He'd read about the kettle bell and how effective it was and had been excited about trying it. That is, until he actually had the kettle bell and the program in his possession. Then it suddenly lacked all appeal.

"I thought you were really excited about these kettle bell exercises," I said.

"I was."

"So how come you haven't tried using the one I got you?"

"I don't know. I think I might return it for a heavier one."

"Right." I rolled my eyes. The idea that he wasn't going to use this particular piece of exercise equipment because it might not be challenging enough was laughable and what I couldn't help but view as a typical male response. Thus, after a mere ten months, I broke it out of the box and decided to use it myself. The program dictates exercising three times a week, for only twenty minutes at a time, which is my kind of commitment when you're talking about an exercise regimen. And, I thought, I can surely do anything for twenty minutes.

The instructor of the program spoke with a Canadian accent that I for some reason associated with perpetual innocence. And while he was very fit and I believe the exercises were effective, he struggled with basic counting or making sure that both sides of the body received equal attention. He went on tangents, which resulted in ten seconds of an exercise on one leg but two minutes on the other side. This was more endearing than annoying, and you could tell when someone behind the camera tried to get him back on track, because he said out loud to himself, "Okay, focus, trainer!" before catching back up with the program.

The kettle bell is a small metal ball with a handle on the top. It is compact and extremely effective. The program involves a series of exercises using the weight, sometimes standing, sometimes sitting. During one of the exercises when you lie on your back, the instructor took great pains to explain that when you're finished with one arm and need to switch to the other side, you first sit up, then switch the kettle bell to the other hand, then lie back down. I wondered why he made such a point of illustrating this method—until I tried to take a short cut. When you're lying on your back exhausted, it seems much easier to pass the kettle bell over your chest from one side to the other, rather than doing a full sit up first. That is, until you whack yourself in the head or groin or, as I managed to, the breast, which you inevitably do because your arms are shaky and gelatinous from the exercises you've just completed. It only takes injuring yourself with the kettle bell one time before you realize the wisdom in making sure the kettle bell will fully clear your body before you pass it from one hand to the other. And for the record, punching yourself in the boob with a heavy metal weight is not a great way to start off the day.

The kettle bell did firm my abs, but it did little to eradicate the layer of fat *covering* my extremely firm abs. I came to peace with the fact that I may never have a perfectly toned body and stopped asking myself if I'd ever get there. If my daughters thought the idea of me being as big as a house was on par with a winged giraffe clad in pink, we were doing just fine.

* * *

CHAPTER SIX

In the Ghetto

"Mom?" Emilia said. "Do you want to hear about my dream?"

"Of course I want to hear about your dream," I answered. "Tell me."

"It was about a little girl with a big crown."

"That's nice."

"Yeah, and then the bad guy came and shot her and blood came out and she died and then he shot her with an arrow and all her blood spilled on the ground. That was the end."

"Oh, um, okay." I'm not sure how to respond to this type of conversation, other than to say "I'm sorry" because I take full responsibility for any morbid thoughts or dreams that my children experience. They get these entirely from me. A fascination with crime and horror and morbidity runs in my family but is completely absent on my husband's side.

Later that day, Mike flipped through the mail before suddenly exclaiming, "Oh no!" My first thought was that someone was suing us. Not that we deserve to be sued or have any reason to be sued, but Mike is in real estate, which means that while many of his peers are wonderful, rational people, others behave like two-year-olds. Two-year-olds with court privileges. We'd been sued before, and I could only attribute the "oh no" to the fact that it was happening again.

"Is someone suing us?" I asked with dread.

He looked at me. "No. No one's suing us. Why's that the first thing you think of?"

"Because it's what scares me."

"Oh. No, it's not a lawsuit. I have jury duty."

"Oh, man! *I* want jury duty."

"Amanda, do you know how weird that makes you?" he asked.

"Come on, it's your civic duty and all that. Plus, it could be a cool trial."

"Ugh," he groaned. "And how is it that I have jury duty for two months?"

"What are you talking about?" I snatched the card from his hand. "It should only be for two weeks." That was the period of time for which I'd last had jury duty. I served on a trial, a case that was a confusion of wrongful termination and sexual harassment from all sides. Another time, I lamentably wasn't chosen. But Mike was right. His jury duty notice stipulated that he be available for up to two months. This seemed terribly unfair, like he had a front-row seat to my all-time favorite show, and I was prohibited from going.

"Ooh, this must be a good one." I did little to hide my envy.

"I can't have jury duty for two months. It'll royally screw up everything."

Mike works an unreal number of hours. If the rest of us attempted to work as hard or as long as people like Mike, we'd likely die of a heart attack inside of a week. He is more driven and hardworking than anyone else I've met. This may sound like an awesome set of traits to have in a husband. And it is, unless you just want to sit on the couch and watch a movie, or take the occasional day off and play hookie. Mike is not good at these things. The guilt over lost productivity is too much for him to bear. He's the type of guy who gets up at four or five in the morning just to get in some extra work before the kids wake up. The idea of two months of jury duty caused him pure panic.

"Maybe I can get out of it because it would be too much of a hardship," he mused.

"Good luck with that," I said.

"What do you mean?"

"Every time I've had jury duty, there are a handful of people who claim that they can't serve because they're business owners and can't sustain the loss of income. The judge will just tell you to work at nights and on the weekends."

"But I *already* work nights and weekends."

"I'm just telling you how it's going to play out."

"That's crazy," he said.

"Not really. Think about it. No one has time to spare. I know it would devastate you to miss that much time to serve on a jury, but everyone has things they can't miss. You just have to make it work."

"There has to be a way to get out of it," he said.

"Well, yes. There are two surefire ways to get out of jury duty."

"Okay." He brightened. "What are they?"

"One is to be a breastfeeding mother."

"Oh. What's the second?"

"To be the sole caregiver for someone dependent on you. Like someone in a wheelchair or otherwise handicapped."

He looked at me with hopeful eyes.

"No," I said. "I forbid you."

"Oh, come on."

"No, Mike. Do not tell them your wife is severely handicapped. You'll get caught, and if you don't get caught, then I'll turn you in."

"You suck."

After his first day serving, I asked him how it went.

"Fine," he said. "I just really hope they don't pick me."

"Do you know what the case is yet?"

"Remember that guy who shot his wife's lover in the Walgreen's parking lot?"

"Shut up!"

"I'm serious. That's the case."

"I would kill to be on a case like that," I said.

"And I love you, but I'm pretty sure that makes you a really terrible person."

"I know," I conceded.

As was expected, Mike reported to jury duty for a few days before he was excused with a free pass for the next two years. The eventual verdict was guilty. The rational, mildly compassionate, adult me knows that this case was a horrible tragedy, but I would still have loved to have been on the jury. It's not that I want people to die or suffer, but they will, regardless of what I want. So if that's going to be the case, I want to witness and participate in the workings of the justice system.

While driving to the store one day, I noticed that a house a few down from ours was taped off with yellow crime-scene tape. Five police cruisers and a crime-scene van sat outside. I restrained the urge to park and ask if I could ride in the van. A dozen police officers stared at me as I drove by. I instantly felt more guilty than curious, as if I was responsible for whatever had taken place, simply because they were staring at me. *Maybe they're keeping a sharp eye out in case the culprit returns to the scene of the crime,* I thought, *because that happens a lot on television and therefore must be true.*

It turned out I wasn't responsible, which was good because I hope to make it through life without ever murdering another human being. An elderly woman who lived alone was found dead in the home. There had also been a fire. Bits of gossip mixed with fact trickled through the neighborhood, and we first thought the fire had killed the woman. We later learned that the cause of death was more likely the hammer found embedded in her head. The neighborhood collectively locked its doors and considered the fact that there might be a killer on the loose. As more gossip filtered through town and residents pressed their connections in law enforcement for information, we learned that the culprit was likely one of the woman's sons. A troubled son, one with a history of drug use, one who probably asked her for money, and perhaps after years of this behavior, she decided to put her foot down and stand firm. And so he killed her. We assumed he then set the house on fire in an attempt to cover the crime, though not much of the home burned. We also learned that the house had been set on fire *before* she died. Had he set the fire while she was asleep? Had she caught him in the act, and he then panicked and picked up the hammer? It was troubling and confusing and scary and sad. We also learned that the son had likely been living with his mother, which meant a killer lived just down the street from us. We wondered why he hadn't been arrested but then reminded ourselves that the reality of our justice system does not work as fast as an episode of *Law & Order*. A week after the murder, the home was set on fire again, and again it failed to burn. Was he attempting to destroy more evidence? Was he the worst arsonist on the planet?

With all the fretting over a murderer in the neighborhood, my in-laws regrettably failed to remember to lock their bikes one night. My father-in-law woke early during a visit and left to walk his dog. Thirty seconds later, he walked back in the house, slammed the door, and yelled, "Fuck!" I'm more likely to use this type of language than he is, and I was taken aback by it. I was about to reprimand him for the outburst while the children were in the house, but then I realized that the matter must have been serious for him to say something like that. "The bikes are gone!" he announced to the house at large. Nana quickly emerged.

"The bikes are gone?" she asked.

"The bikes are gone," he confirmed.

"Gone where?"

"Gone from the bike rack. They've been *stolen*."

"The bikes have been stolen?"

"The bikes have been stolen."

"You didn't *lock* them?" she asked.

At this point, my father-in-law's face began to redden. He realized that he hadn't locked the bikes and that worse than their theft was that he felt responsible for their theft. During tense moments like these, I typically stand very still and hold my breath, almost as if the negativity is like a bad case of the hiccups, and if I hold my breath long enough, it will dissipate. Eventually I had to breathe again and tried to offer some consolation. "You know what the bright side is?" I asked. "Now you guys get to go shopping. You get to go buy *new* bikes. Won't that be *fun?*"

"Those *were* new bikes," Papa said.

I went back to holding my breath.

* * *

The next day, a package arrived at our front door but was addressed to our friend Kelly. He'd recently purchased a home of his own in Boise and no longer needed to stay with us when in town. I called him and told him there was a package at our house for him.

"Thanks," he said. "I'll pick it up today. There should be two or three more arriving in the next few days."

"Kelly, you have your own place now. Why are you still having packages sent to us? Is it your crazy HCG injections? Is it illegal drugs? Is it porn? Are you trafficking in porn and trying to cover your tracks by sending it to our house? We have children! How could you do such a thing?"

"Calm down." He laughed. "I promise it's all very innocent." He proceeded to tell me about the items he purchased and had shipped to my house, and all I heard were words like mega trans reaction converter mechanism. My brain ached, so I stopped him.

"Kelly, please don't say another word about what these things are. I've decided I don't really want to know. But why are you having them shipped here?"

"Well, I just don't think it would be safe on my street. If a package sits outside my door all day, I'm pretty sure it's going to grow legs and disappear. I just don't trust my neighborhood."

"Are you kidding me? Our neighborhood is *way* more ghetto than yours. We just had some bikes stolen, and we had a murder on our street. There's no way you can beat that."

"All right, Amanda. You win. You're more ghetto than me. I'm still having stuff shipped to your house."

"Fine. But you can only ship your weird geeky computer nuclear reactor crap. No drugs and no porn."

"Deal."

In truth, it's hard to feel ghetto in Boise, Idaho. Anyone who feels ghetto or threatened in Boise needs to go spend some time in a big city. I worked in Baltimore for a few years. You can't convince me there's much ghetto in Idaho. There's a little bit, of course. We have our meth heads and trashy people, but I'm pretty sure you'll find them anywhere.

The most ghetto I've felt in Idaho was when my kids were sick on a Sunday and I took them to the clinic inside the downtown Rite-Aid. And it wasn't my surroundings that were ghetto; *I* was ghetto. I'm not typically ghetto, but when your children behave abominably in a drugstore or Walmart, and you find yourself snapping at them in harsh tones spoken too loud, and every sentence ends in *"right now,"* even the classiest citizen is suddenly ghetto. And I'm not all that classy to begin with.

I take my kids to the doctor far more often than could possibly be necessary. This seems ridiculous, until you're the person that *doesn't* take their kid to the doctor when she really needed to go. You only have to be that parent once before you learn your lesson and decide to err on the side of caution ever after. This happened with Ivy when she was two. I noticed she sounded congested when I picked her up from daycare. By bedtime, she was definitely ill, but nothing seemed *serious*, so we dosed her with infant Ibuprofen and hoped for the best.

At ten o'clock, the coughing and crying began. At the beginning of a difficult night with a sick child, we are attentive parents and scurry to our children's bedsides to soothe what ails them and tuck them in again. By two a.m., we elbow each other for a full minute, trying to do it in a casual way so that it seems less like *It's your turn to deal with the kid* and more like *I rolled over in my sleep, and my elbow grazed your ribs, but now that you're awake, perhaps you want to be the better parent and check on our child while I drift back into blissful slumber.* My technique failed on the night in question, so at two in the morning, I got up with Ivy, consoling myself with the fact that at that moment I was indeed the better parent, and spent a few hours sitting on the couch with her, trying to keep her upright so that she might sleep better. *This is one bitch of a cold*, I thought. The next morning, I called the pediatrician and told them she had some labored breathing.

"Why don't you go ahead and bring her in right now," they suggested.

Wow, I thought. *What great customer service! They're so accommodating.* Beyond the desire to serve their patients well, though, they were more concerned with the fact that a two-year-old was having trouble breathing. When she was examined by a doctor, I mentioned our middle-of-the-night ordeal.

"You know," I said, "at one point, it was maybe two in the morning, I actually thought about taking her to the emergency room."

I expected to be told that that wouldn't have been necessary. Instead, the doctor replied with: "Yes, that's what you should have done."

It turns out that Ivy had pneumonia and that when a child makes weird wheezing noises and struggles to breathe, you shouldn't wait until the pediatrician's office opens up in the morning. Ivy was admitted to the hospital where she recovered far more quickly than my guilty conscience. Part of her speedy recovery involved her innate ability to chug liquids.

"We're going to need to give her intravenous fluids," the nurse advised.

"That won't be necessary," I said.

"You don't understand," explained the nurse. "Dehydration is a real threat, and kids aren't able to keep up with drinking as much fluid as they need."

"What do you want her to drink?" I asked.

"It's not that simple."

"I'm serious," I said. "What would she have to drink right now in order for us to forgo the IV?"

She shot skepticism my way but placed two bottles of Pedialyte on a table.

"Crack those suckers open," I said. "Do you have a straw?"

She opened the first bottle and handed it to me with a straw. She turned her back then and began removing the seal from the second bottle.

Ivy was half asleep but perked up when I commanded, "Drink this."

The nurse turned back to us. I handed her the empty Pedialyte bottle, which Ivy had drained like a freshman at a frat party.

"Mom?" Ivy asked. "Can I have more?"

"Oh," said the nurse. "I've never seen a two-year-old do that before."

"Yes." I smiled. "She gets it from me."

So when the girls displayed cold symptoms and complained of ear pain on a Sunday morning, I decided to take them to the clinic. I hate the clinic, but it's better to go than to force my kids to suffer with ear infections and strep throat. There are two doctors we've seen on previous visits to the Rite-Aid clinic. One is a kind elderly woman who takes great care with her patients and pride in her job. The other is a younger man who appears to detest people and working with them, which makes me wonder if he's really invested in making them any better. We ended up with him. His mouth is a permanent frown, and he ignores children when they speak to him. But my kids did have ear infections, and we suffered through his demeanor and got our prescriptions for the necessary antibiotics. Since I was already in a pharmacy, it seemed ludicrous to take the prescription somewhere else, but that's what I should have done. A downtown pharmacy is not a pleasant place. I should have driven to a nice, clean Rite-Aid on the outskirts of town, but I didn't. I put on my ghetto face and stood in line with cranky children. We dropped the prescription off and then had half an hour to kill inside the Rite-Aid. No problem, I thought. We'll look at toys, meander the aisles, and count squares of linoleum. But Ivy was at an age where she could pull things off of shelves faster than I could return them. And they didn't want to peruse soft, plushy toys or board games; they wanted to manhandle barbecue lighters and glass bottles of perfume and windshield washer fluid. My parenting manifested into a steady stream of "Don't touch that, stop it right now" and constant threats to count to five. I'm not sure why this works or what my children think will happen should I ever reach the full count of five before they comply with my demands, but I'll continue with the numbers game for as long as it is effective.

"Mommy, I have to go potty," Emilia said.

"Great! Let's go potty." Suddenly a bathroom in a downtown pharmacy seemed like a wonderful place to take the children. At least it didn't have the potential threats of the rest of the store. Nor did it have five hundred thousand items that my two-year-old wanted to rip from the shelves. I held them each by the hand and dragged them to the back of the store. We found a restroom, but it was locked. *This is a good thing,* I thought, *because a locked restroom implies some level of control over who uses that restroom, thereby decreasing the chances that we will encounter a hypodermic needle or used condom.*

We went back to the front of the store and waited in line behind a girl who couldn't have been older than fourteen. She was buying cigarettes, Red Bull, and a pregnancy test from the slowest cashier on the planet, who didn't bat an eye at the purchases of the customer before us. When it was our turn, we approached the cashier.

"Hi, we just need the key for the restroom."

"Oh, well you didn't need to wait in line for that, sweetie," she said. A nametag pinned to her shirt read Tabby. "You don't get the key from me. I wish I would have known. I could have told you so that you didn't have to spend all that time waiting here in line. Your little one probably needs to go real bad, don't you, sweetie?" she said, looking at Ivy.

"No," Emilia corrected. "*I* need to use the potty. Ivy is my sister but she sometimes has accidents but I pee on the potty every time and we came for the medicine because the office where I was born with the doctor there is closed on the Sunday."

"Oh," said Tabby. "And how old are you?"

Sweet Jesus, just give me the fucking key.

"Mom!" Emilia looked up at me. "I really have to go potty."

"Yes, perhaps we can continue this conversation later. Can you just tell me where to get the key?"

"Right," said Tabby, "because you were waiting in line for it. But next time you'll know you don't get the bathroom key from me. If you need to use the restroom, you just go…" She trailed off then, distracted by a fly. "Those darn things are always getting in here."

"Where's the bathroom key?" I demanded.

She looked annoyed then, followed by hurt that I didn't want to discuss the nuisance of flies.

"I told you, you get the key from the pharmacy," she said.

"No, you didn't tell me," I snapped. "And for the record, if my kid pisses on your floor, it's your fault."

I chastised myself for letting the ghetto of my surroundings infect me. My use of the word "pisses" when speaking to a stranger was a clear indication that that's what was happening. I dragged my kids back over to the pharmacy where I was immediately told that my prescription wasn't yet ready.

"I know. I just need the key for the bathroom."

"Here." He handed me a wooden block the size of a skateboard, attached to a small key. I herded the kids back to the bathroom. We let ourselves in to an unbelievable stench, the sort of smell I imagine invades the latrines at military outposts.

"Oh my god," I said. "All right, let's do this fast."

"I can do it, Mom," Emilia said, pushing her shorts and undies down and hoisting herself up.

"No wait!" The toilet seat was covered in drops of moisture. One would assume this is errant urine, but who knows? It could have been anything. I wiped the toilet seat down in haste and then lined it with clean bits of toilet paper, all of which fell off as I put Emilia on the seat.

"Mommy," said Ivy. "This is my shirt?" I turned then to see Ivy pick up a disgusting piece of fabric that may or may not have at one time been an article of clothing. It had been shoved in a corner of the bathroom and could have been what the staff used to clean the toilet.

"Don't touch that!" I snapped. Ivy began to cry.

"What's this, Mom?" I turned back to Emilia to see her standing next to the toilet, shorts and undies still down around her ankles, holding an unopened can of one of those energy-drink-plus-booze concoctions, which I tend to think of as alcohol for teenagers, because no self-respecting adult would drink something so clearly marketed to underage drinkers. If anyone had snapped a picture of Emilia at that moment, my parental shame would have been complete.

"Where did you get that?" I asked above Ivy's increasing wail. "Put that down!"

"It was right there." She indicated the floor next to the toilet.

"Did you go potty?" I asked.

"Um, probably I don't need to go," she said.

"You've got to be kidding," I muttered. "Okay, let's just get out of here." I pulled up Emilia's shorts, picked up Ivy, despite her ongoing tantrum, and we left the bathroom and all its glory behind. I went back to the pharmacy to return the key.

"I think your restroom is in need of attention," I said. "Especially the unopened can of *alcohol* that's stashed beside the toilet." I'm not known for emphasizing the word alcohol as if it's a bad thing, but in this case it seemed entirely merited.

"Okay," said the pharmacist, who was clearly not surprised to hear this. Was it his? Did he and Tabby meet on break to share a forty ounce of cherry-flavored malt liquor?

The next time my children are sick on a Sunday and we're forced to visit the clinic, I'm going to embrace the ghetto instead of battling with it. I'll accomplish this by wearing pajama pants, slippers, and a tank top that's so tight it highlights both my tramp stamp in the back and my overhanging belly in the front. I'll feed my kids Hostess products and Slim Jims while we wait for their prescriptions. Our ghetto will be complete, if only for a day.

* * *

CHAPTER SEVEN

Career Day

"And what is it that you do?"

The woman posing this question was strikingly pretty, so much so that it made me uncomfortable. She was pure grace and poise, with slender, delicate limbs and a voice of honey. Her perfect pale skin was in stark contrast to her dark hair, which included no sign of frizz or flyaways. My head reeked of psoriasis medication. I reminded myself that in addition to being beautiful, she was also a librarian and must therefore share my love of books.

"I'm a *writer*," I said with far too much emphasis.

"What do you write?" She smiled with perfect teeth and Revlon lips.

I glanced nervously toward the door. The elementary school library where I was volunteering for the day was perhaps not the best place to discuss my titles. I didn't want my daughter's classmates to overhear and report to their parents that during library time they discussed a book called

This Little Piggy Went to the Liquor Store. I pictured Emilia being shunned from play dates and birthday parties because of her mother's vulgarity.

"I write humor," I said as a group of second-graders filed in. I heard a ridiculous and strange quality in my voice, one that spoke of trying too hard and being intimidated by another's physical beauty.

I knew I wasn't coming across well when, over the next half hour, the librarian kept referring to the fact that I'm a writer. "Well, you'll be good at shelving books, since you're a *writer*," she'd say. I shut my mouth, tackled the Dewey decimal system in earnest, and consoled myself with the thought that perfect-looking people are cursed. I feel terribly sad for them, as their beauty throws the dynamics of every situation off balance. Luckily, I don't have to worry about such problems, and instead I like to make people uncomfortable through vulgar speech and grossly inappropriate behavior. I didn't volunteer in the library again.

When my children ask what I do, I tell them Mommy's a writer and that I write books for adults to read. They then re-engineer this statement and tell people that their mommy writes adult books, which sometimes makes it sound like I write porn. That would be just a bit funny and ironic and uncomfortable, except for the fact that I have a penname under which I write porn.

I find explaining to my children what I do much easier than reading reviews of what I do. It's one thing to have your writing criticized, but another when anonymous masses attack your character. I've been called an alcoholic, a horrible parent, an animal abuser, and an angry bitch. I wouldn't bristle if those were all true, but I can really only concede to 50 percent at best. Luckily, I'm fairly thick-skinned and full of myself, so I don't let these things get to me too much. I have writer friends who will plunge into an emotional funk that will last for months over one bad review. Not only are writers emotional, but we also vary in terms of forecasting our success, which on any given day might be ridiculous expectations of fame and wealth and validation, or complete doom and gloom accompanied by razor blades and cheap whiskey.

As we geared up for our trip to Mexico, during which I would spend three months in close quarters with not only my husband and children, but also my in-laws, I pounced on an opportunity to get away by myself, if only for one night, to attend a writers' retreat. These are good for writers on many levels. Not just for inspiration and motivation and to ensure that we get out of bed, bathe, and interact with other humans, but also to remind ourselves that no matter how ridiculous and crazy we are, there's always someone out there who's weirder and even more out of touch with reality.

The writers' retreat had a wonderful mix of overconfidence and low self-esteem. The day of writing exercises and critiques included praising one another's work or finding delicate ways of saying, "That's crap." The latter was usually accomplished when one writer would tell another that while her story was excellent, perhaps she should consider changing the title, plot, characters, setting, and theme.

After receiving a critique from a writer who suggested I change my title, plot, characters, setting, and theme, I retired to the guestroom of a neighboring cabin. To say *cabin* is to give a false impression, though. When I think of a cabin, I think of a scary, bug-infested place, cold and dirty and uninviting, much like the cabin my grandparents took me to for a summer of my youth in Maine. I associate it with old people and old items, like thirty-year-old crocheted doilies and antique toilet brushes. A cabin is not a true cabin unless you walk in, immediately contemplate finding a Super 8, and realize that you are in what would be a perfect setting for a horror film. For people of my generation, a cabin is a place where beautiful teenagers in tight clothing go to lose their virginity and be savagely dismembered or impaled.

The cabin at the writers' retreat, however, is what people with *money* refer to as a cabin. It has design elements that harken to nature and rural life, but with state-of-the-art appliances, travertine tiles, granite countertops, jetted tubs, steam showers, and heated marble floors. And no one gets murdered there. This cabin was so off the charts that the bed I slept in was actually too sophisticated for me to make the following morning. I struggled with it for about forty minutes, circling back and forth from one side of the bed to the other, pulling at various corners of fabric and hoping they would magically make sense again. I was unable to decipher how to deal with the extra pocket at the top of the bedspread. Or was it a duvet? Should I put the pillows inside of that part? Was it a hiding place for sex toys or dead hookers? Why had I not paid attention to the intricacies of the bed when I'd gotten into it the night before?

I abandoned the bed and assumed that there would be some sort of staff who cleaned the cabin and had fancy-bed-making certifications. They would certainly know how to deal with it, and if I wasted any more time, I might miss out on a cheese-filled pastry.

I mingled with those I hadn't met the day before, writers both new and known, and realized that each of us walked around with our own level of crazy. And I'm okay with crazy as long as it's my particular *brand* of crazy. We're all nuts, but some people are a different brand of nuts, and those are the ones you need to watch out for. For instance, the nuts with obese egos, questionable hygiene, and/or the inability to correctly interact with other people are a brand to which I am severely allergic.

I find the company of most writers enjoyable. They are odd but interesting, fascinating but not frightening. Fantasy and science fiction writers, specifically, are an odd lot. I don't know anyone who would disagree with this, especially the writers themselves. In and among the fantasy and science fiction writers I've met lurk the most intelligent and insightful people I've ever encountered. When meeting one, the trick is to as quickly as possible ascertain if you are dealing with a complete whack job, a genius, or most likely, some combination of the two. One science fiction writer I know keeps me apprised of the workings or failings of his dog's bowel movements. I have never met the dog. I have no connection with the dog. But this information is communicated to me regularly, via email, text, and Facebook. I'd almost written him off as a complete whack job until I read his work, at which point I ascribed him a certain amount of genius thrown in the mix.

Humor writers are some of the most troubled people I've met. It makes sense when you think about it, because nothing slays childhood trauma, horrific demons, and devastating insecurity like a good knock-knock joke. Conversely, people who write about troubling subject matter are some of the most well-balanced. It makes me think that you really can't judge a book by its cover. Or a writer, for that matter. Just like serial killers. Both Bundy and Dahmer looked like pleasant fellows, and by appearances, the BTK killer could have been an encyclopedia salesman. Typical clues of human nature are so often counterintuitive that I fear telling someone I write humor, for they will naturally assume I torture small animals and keep kidnapped transients in a secret room in my basement. Henceforth, I shall refrain from telling people that I write humor. I'll lie and say I write horror in the hopes that they will ascribe me some level of normalcy. Another benefit of telling people you write horror as opposed to humor is that you remove all pressure to be funny and are instead free to brood about all of the horrible things in the world, which is one of my favorite pastimes.

At the writers' retreat, I found that a good measure of the quality of someone's writing lies in how much, or little, they talk about it. For example, if you ask someone what they write, and they answer, "Short stories," or, "I'm working on a young adult novel," they might be writing something worth reading. Conversely, if a writer answers that they are working on a "paranormal trilogy about an all-women's softball team who secretly battles a demon mafia, and the main character's name is Quinoa, and they live in a world where people mate in zero-gravity bubbles launched into space, so there's a bit of a love story in there, too," you should run away. Excessive babbling on about a book is often a good indicator that the book is lacking in some way, or the writer is experiencing diarrhea of the mouth in an attempt to compensate for crippling insecurity.

Just when I feel I've gotten past this stage, that I've somehow transcended the social oddities common to many writers, or sufficiently beat my own crippling insecurities into submission, I meet an intimidating librarian and practically scream at her that "I'm a *writer!*" The next time someone asks what I do, maybe I'll answer, "I'm a dork," and put the matter immediately to rest.

* * *

CHAPTER EIGHT

Sandi's Got Talent

"Okay, Ivy. I learned a new game called Simon Says," said Emilia.

"Okay."

"And I'm going to tell you what to do, and you're going to do it."

"Okay."

"But only if Simon says."

"Okay."

"Simon says touch your toes."

Ivy touched her toes.

"Simon says turn around."

Ivy turned around.

"Stand on one foot."

Ivy stood on one foot.

"No, Ivy. You're only supposed to do it if Simon says."

"Okay."

This same conversation and scene repeated itself two more times before I saw Ivy's tiny brow begin to furrow and her fists ball in frustration. Her posture suggested she might take a swing at her sister.

"Girls, maybe you should play a different game," I said.

"No," they barked at me in unison.

"Fine." I walked into the kitchen to locate my ringing phone. "Hey, Sandi, what's up?"

"I want you to mark your calendar because there's an event coming up that I want you guys to come to. It's like a talent competition, and my band is playing."

"Your Mom Band?"

"I'm not in any other bands, so yes, my Mom Band."

"What's the event?"

"It's like a work thing."

"Like a realtor thing?"

"Yes."

"So it's like a realtor talent show?"

"Yes."

"Wow, that sounds really... interesting."

"Promise me you'll come."

I promised, of course, and told her I would line up a baby-sitter. Then I saw Ivy bend over and charge her sister, ramming Emilia in the gut with her head. This was in response to Emilia's repeated remark that Ivy was "doing it wrong" when it came to playing Simon Says.

"I have to go," I told Sandi, "but send me the details, and I'll make sure we're there."

I hung up the phone and returned to Emilia and Ivy in the living room.

"Mom," Emilia whined. "Ivy's not playing the game right."

"I know, but she doesn't understand how this game works, so maybe we should play a different game."

"Okay," Emilia said. "How about Big-Assed Statues?"

"Wait, *what?*" Surely I hadn't heard her correctly.

"Big-Eyed Statues. It's fun. Watch." She then proceeded to strike a pose and freeze with wide eyes.

"That's really good, Emilia. How about you, Ivy? Let me see your big-eyed statue."

Ivy followed suit, and I decided that Big-Eyed Statues is the best game on the planet. It requires no parts or mess. No one touches or injures anyone else, and it's completely silent. Mike entered the room then and saw the girls in their frozen poses.

"What are you doing?" he asked.

"We're playing Big-Assed Statues," Emilia said.

"*What?*"

"They're playing Big-*Eyed* Statues," I explained.

"Oh, okay," he said. "For a second, I thought she said something else."

"Let's play a new game," Emilia suggested.

Nana walked in the house then and solved the problem by producing a bag of balloons. Next to Big-Assed Statues, playing with balloons is easily my second favorite game. Though it occasionally ends in injury, I still think balloons are fun, even as a grown woman. And they're cheap. I blew up two balloons, and Nana and I sat on the couch watching the girls play. That's another great thing about balloons; the girls require minimal effort from me. At best, I have to tap a floating balloon back in their direction. Emilia's method of play was hitting the balloon up in the air and then seeing how long she could keep it going before it touched the ground. She giggled like the little girl she is and seemed perfectly content. Ivy's method of play was more brutal and did a good job of highlighting their differences. She dove onto the balloon, punched it, tried to sit on it, and pantomimed killing it, though it miraculously survived. While Emilia continued giggling, Ivy emitted a series of grunts and battle cries. Both girls at one point smashed into the coffee table. Emilia whimpered for a moment and then came to me for a hug, which I believe is a perfectly appropriate reaction for how hard she hit her head. Ivy, hitting with the same force, simply wobbled for a moment like a cartoon character before resuming her game of Kill the Balloon.

Emilia lost her balance then and toppled over in the sort of graceless maneuver that she could only have inherited from me. The expression on her face made Nana laugh. It was one of those times when your laughter comes spontaneously and there's nothing you can do to stop. Emilia picked herself up, looked Nana dead in the eye with a frown, and then grabbed her balloon and repeatedly hit Nana in the face with it.

"Okay, okay," I intervened. "Maybe we should go back to Big-Assed Statues."

"To what?" Nana asked.

"I mean, Big-Eyed Statues. It's fun and silent, and no one will end up with stitches."

"Hey, I had stitches. Nana, look at my owie." Emilia showcased a sizable scar on her forehead and appeared to have forgiven the previous moment.

The stitches were the result of an accident on an evening during which I'd miraculously not had a drop of alcohol. It's safe to say that on most evenings, chances are I've had at least one drink. But on this particular night, I was holding off, not wanting the sedative effects of alcohol to dampen my work ethic. I sat at the dining room table working while Mike took the girls into the bathroom to assist in the brushing of teeth. After a few seconds, I heard a thump followed by a scream. Parents become strangely intuitive to the sounds of the thump alone. We can tell what the likely severity of the accident will be just by this sound because we know the sound of a child's body during a harmless fall, and anything with a different quality from this sound may be cause for greater alarm. The scream that follows usually confirms our suspicions. I rose from the table and went to the bathroom where Mike handed Emilia to me.

"She fell pretty hard," he said.

"That's what it sounded like." I carried Emilia out to the couch to try to comfort her. As soon as we sat down, I knew this would be an emergency room visit. "It's a pretty big gash," I said to Mike. "I think I'm going to have to take her in."

"I don't think so," Mike said. "I think she just scraped it."

"No, I'm looking right at it. I'm telling you this is a big one."

This was one of those moments where one rational adult refuses to believe what another rational adult tells them, for no apparent reason. "Well," Mike called above Emilia's continued cries, "the light in the living room is really bad. Let me get a flashlight." That was perhaps one of the most ridiculous statements my husband has ever uttered, as dim lighting does not make one hallucinate a giant gash in their child's forehead, but I stopped trying to convince him and decided to let the wound speak for itself. He came to us with a flashlight, trailed by a silent and watchful Ivy. He approached with the lit flashlight but then said, "Oh," and turned it off. "Yeah, that's a doozy."

"I'll take her in. Tell me what happened because they're going to ask."

"She was stepping up on the stepstool, but not really paying attention, and she missed. Her head hit on the step."

"Okay, we'll be back."

It was almost nine o'clock at night, and Emilia calmed down by the time we got in the car, recognizing that despite her new injury, she was getting to go on a late-night adventure with Mommy. Suddenly a huge and painful gash in the forehead seemed like a great idea. We drove the five minutes to the hospital and parked outside the emergency room. From my own childhood with a Thanksgiving Day broken arm, I remembered emergency rooms as places with creepy people, nauseating smells, and uncomfortable chairs, where you had to wait for hours and fill out excessive paperwork. This was no longer the case, at least not in Boise. A large, beautiful fish tank sat right inside the door, with not a single dead fish floating at the top, which for some reason I always expect. We were seen within minutes. A ghetto girl who had been waiting next to us complained of back pain in order to get drugs of some sort. This may seem like a callous assumption, but this girl was an atrocious liar, and I wanted to tell her to take an acting class before her next emergency room visit.

During our entire time in the hospital, which was less than two hours, I was asked about twenty times to explain what had happened. Emilia was asked five times. They wanted to make sure we had our stories straight and that no one was abusing this innocent little girl. I'm glad they do this. I *understand* why they do this. Ironically, I want to beat child abusers to death. I honestly do. But when you're the person being examined with such scrutiny, it's difficult. *Can't they tell I'm a good person?* I thought. They also pulled up the sleeves and legs of Emilia's pajamas to ensure she didn't have any telltale bruises or other injuries indicative of abuse.

When they were convinced that I am not, in fact, one of those people whom I want to personally kill, they got ready for stitches. Part of this process involved wrapping Emilia in a sheet to keep her still so that she wouldn't flail her arms and legs or try to punch the doctor in the face. This tactic would have been entirely necessary if Ivy had been on the table, but not with Emilia. I wanted to tell them that Emilia would comply with anything they told her to do, that she would in all probability be the most ideal patient they'd ever encountered. But I figured they probably hear things like this all the time, so we wrapped her up in a sheet. Emilia thought it was fun; I told her she was my little eggroll. As I expected, she lay there still and silent, gritting her teeth but not wanting to disappoint any of the adults around her. I could tell that what she was going through was painful. After all, no one likes repeated needles in their forehead, but Emilia did everything she could not to cry. I kept my face an inch from hers but out of the way of the doctor and told her everything was going to be okay. I told her what a great job she was doing and that I was so proud of her for being so brave. I told her it was okay for her to cry, because it broke my heart to see such a stoic little girl.

"Mama?" she said when the doctor was about halfway through.

"Yes?"

"I love you," she whispered. I didn't know that children were capable of this, but it must be instinct. When you think you might not survive, you tell those you love how you feel about them.

"I love you, too, Emilia, but you're going to be just fine. The doctor's almost done."

And when it was all said and done, Emilia had a Frankenstein-like wound on her head to be proud of, complete with five stitches. She showed it off at school and only wavered a little when it was time to return to the hospital to have them removed, though I assured her that taking stitches out was not painful and nothing like when you have them put in.

The girls in this family are tough. Ivy is a bulldog, and while Emilia may be delicate, as little girls often are, she's incredibly strong when the situation is serious or, in this case, when someone binds you so that you are incapable of moving and approaches your head with hooked needles. Their cousins are scrappy, Nana is the most badass grandmother I know, and Aunt Sandi is the toughest four-foot-ten realtor you'll ever meet.

Sandi's brass balls came in handy during the talent competition. It was a realtor event, which meant that a lot of her colleagues and work associates were in the room. When she arrived, she thought that it was basically a realtor version of *America's Got Talent*. Actually, the realtors comprised the audience, not the other talent acts that Sandi's Mom Band would compete against. If Sandi had been in competition with the other realtors, she would have kicked ass. She knew this, which is why she'd been excited about it. But it turned out that Sandi's Mom Band was competing against four of the most talented musical groups in Boise, including Andrew Coba who will one day be very famous, as well as an eleven-year-old blues prodigy, and another band comprised of two drop-dead gorgeous, young singers from Nashville with killer voices and original songs.

"Oh shit," Sandi said when she arrived and saw this.

"What's wrong?"

"Well these aren't other realtors. I've seen half of these bands play in town. These are like… *professionals.*"

"You'll do fine," I said, though I had my doubts. I'd heard Sandi sing Karaoke twice before. The first time, she nailed every note and shocked a roomful of people with her incredible pipes. The second time, she'd had a few too many drinks before approaching the Karaoke machine and was entirely off throughout a five-minute song, though drunk enough to be oblivious to it. Because of the number of colleagues that filled the room, I knew she wasn't going to be drunk before taking the stage, so I had every confidence in her singing ability, but she'd also be playing the guitar, something she'd taught herself about three weeks prior. And I had no idea what the skill level was of the other moms in Sandi's Mom Band.

Mike and I bought beer and sat at a table along with Mike's dad. My father-in-law appeared extremely nervous, worried for the fate of his daughter who was about to perform in front of a roomful of intoxicated spectators with scorecards in front of them.

The first band centered around the aforementioned and future-famous Andrew Coba. He was sixteen at the time and in possession of the type of talent that instantly commands a room, without the assistance of ego, falsehood, or anything sparkly. He simply owned raw talent. He made me want to go back in time and spend more of my teen years learning and creating, and less time polishing my Zippo and drinking vodka Slurpees. The second band was a guy/girl duo that you might find playing at a coffee shop. They were good and had a likeable quality, the people you find yourself inexplicably wanting to hug. The third act was the eleven-year-old blues prodigy who played a Stevie Ray Vaughn set. He needed some polishing, but his age and his guitar playing made up for anything lacking. He was the sort of kid who made you realize that no matter what great feats you accomplish in the rest of your life, your opportunity to be a prodigy of anything is long gone. After him, it was time for Sandi and her Mom Band. They'd been practicing together for months but apparently hadn't yet come up with a name. Every time Sandi had mentioned the group in the past, they were just called "my band." A failure to name a band is indicative of the level of confidence in the members. It's sort of like holding off on naming a child because you're just not yet convinced that you want it. The five women took to the stage and fumbled about for a bit, darting nervous glances at one another, as if to say, "Shit, are we really going to do this?" This sort of behavior did little to inspire confidence in the audience regarding the upcoming performance.

Sandi took the microphone and said, "Hi, we're the Mom Band, and we've just been playing together for a few weeks. We have two short songs for you, and then we're outta here." I thought this was a smart move. No one likes a stage hog, and while the audience was looking forward to the entertainment, no one wanted the entertainment to go on *forever*.

But then another one of Sandi's band mates had to put her two cents in, something about the commonalities of stressed working women. Even that was okay until a third band mate started talking. She didn't have much of a point but rambled on, basically rephrasing what the other two had said. Someone in the back of the room shouted, "Play a song already!"

I'm not sure if the talking was an introduction or more of a stall technique. In any case, as soon as they started playing, it appeared that the Mom Band was actually two smaller groups, individual bands, who were sharing the same stage and happened to be playing the same song at the same time. Some had guitars that were plugged in, some did not. One instrument was on key while another was grossly out of tune. I stared at the table in front of me and held Mike's hand in a death grip under the table. It was too painful to watch. "It's going to be okay," Mike whispered. I wondered how my father-in-law was processing it. Was he mortified? Concerned over his daughter's future emotional well-being? He looked relatively calm. The song mercifully ended, but not before Sandi had a brief chance to show off her vocal talents, which were spot on. Then they played their second song, and I cringed when I recognized it as the Indigo Girls. Don't get me wrong; I enjoy the Indigo Girls. They're good. But not every female band on the planet needs to do a cover of "Closer to Fine." The Indigo Girls did a fine job of it themselves, and no garage band on the planet is going to make "Closer to Fine" any closer to fine than the original already is.

The Mom Band finished, and the audience clapped politely. The final act was the duo of young, hot, uber-talented girls from Nashville. I'd hoped maybe they'd just be hot and not so talented, but they stole the show. The men in the room stared with rapt attention while the women in the room felt old and fat. After they finished and the audience applauded loudly, it was time to vote. We had slips of paper in front of us with the names of the acts, and we had to rate them. The first, second, and third-place winners would receive cash prizes. I took a look at the paper in front of me and circled The Mom Band. I turned to Mike to gather his vote and found that he was staring blankly at the paper before him. We'd been married long enough that I could read his dilemma. He *really* wanted to vote for the hot chicks. I watched him for a full minute before I leaned over and whispered. "Mike, you *have* to vote for your sister."

"You're right. That was a close one." He shook himself out of a daze and then dutifully circled The Mom Band like a good brother should. The Mom Band didn't win, of course, though neither did Andrew Coba. The hot chicks took first prize, coffee house pair took second, and blues prodigy took third.

"See," I said to Mike, "you did the right thing. Now we know for sure that your sister's band had at least a few votes in the mix."

"You're right," he said. "Now let's get the hell out of here."

As we stood to leave, I turned to my father-in-law and asked, "Well, what did you think?"

"I was really worried at first, but I thought they did great," he said. "I'm really proud of her." I was amazed by this and attribute it to the fact that he loves his daughter very much, and maybe also because he's hard of hearing.

This event caused me more stress than it did my husband, perhaps because I would rather stand naked in Times Square and do the Macarena than sing in front of a room full of people. I'm the sort of person that tries to get by just mouthing the words during "Happy Birthday." The only time in my life I've enjoyed singing was when my children were babies, did not yet have the capacity for judgment, and I knew they'd have no memory of it when older.

In high school, I auditioned for the school musical. While I was well aware of my vocal deficiencies, I could not stand the thought of being in the audience as opposed to on the stage. "Why do we have to do *musicals?*" I whined to my friends, who had devastatingly beautiful voices and zero empathy. "Why can't we just do straight plays?"

Two days before the audition, I sat at the dining room table with what was then called a boom box. No one else was home. I hit record and put everything I had, short of dumping a bucket of water onto my head, into channeling Irene Cara's "What a Feeling" from *Flashdance*. After recording only ten seconds, I hit stop, rewind, and play. I decided to immediately erase the tape, lest the horrors coming forth from the cassette assault the ears of another human. I rewound and decided to try again. Irene Cara was simply out of my range, I reasoned, and settled instead on "Karma Chameleon." I replayed the ten seconds of my Culture Club impersonation only to discover that my voice through the cassette had no resemblance to the voice in my head, because the voice in my head wasn't great, but it was acceptable. The voice from the cassette was a blight on all things audible. Therefore, the problem was with the recording device, and when I was live and on stage, I'd sound just fine.

The audition involved standing on stage and choking back tears while slaughtering a song that no one else seemed to have any trouble with. This time, I *could* hear that I was off-key, but that didn't mean I could find my way *on*-key. And nothing will make you sound worse than trying not to cry, which added a strange hint of strangulation to the quality of my singing. Nonetheless, I was awarded the glamour of playing the dog in *The Bremen Town Musicians,* though the script was rewritten slightly so that someone else could perform my solo. I believe it was the first time in the history of my high school Drama Department that a script was *rewritten* to avoid hearing a student sing. I'm special that way.

* * *

CHAPTER NINE

The Facial Pivot

You'd think that Alaskans would be natural fans of cold and ice and winter. That they'd be innately inclined to fur-lined fashions and a diet of salted fish. Not so much. Most Alaskans I've met regard cold weather as something to which they are severely allergic. The longer they live in Alaska, the more obsessed they become with finding warm, sunny climates in which they can bronze themselves for their golden years. This is why the farther south you travel, the more Alaskan license plates you'll see.

Years ago, my in-laws began traveling to Mexico every chance they could. When they finally retired from twenty-five years of teaching, they sold their home in Sitka, Alaska, to be able to afford building a home in Mexico. When I tell people this, they incorrectly assume that my in-laws have a lot of money, which is when I realize they weren't listening, because I clearly stated that my in-laws are retired teachers. Not human traffickers or drug mules or even chemistry teachers with really good meth recipes.

In case you haven't heard, teachers are not notoriously well-compensated. When my in-laws first moved to Todos Santos, Mexico, they lived in a small RV parked on a lot they'd purchased. I distinctly recall my father-in-law's pride when he showed me "the facilities," which consisted of a toilet seat glued to the top of a bucket.

"I'm sorry," I whispered to my husband, "but explain to me why he's so proud of the poop bucket?"

"Because it has a seat on it. It's like a *luxury* poop bucket."

"Lord, help us. How long are we staying?"

"Just wait until he shows you the shower. Try to look impressed."

The "shower" he referred to was a bag of water that hung on a hook. These are also known as "sun showers" because the sun heats the water, and because adding the word "sun" to a miserable experience makes it shiny and happy. Think of a really horrible act like stabbing or torture. Sounds awful, right? Add a little sun to it to make it sun stabbing or sun torture. Suddenly it sounds only slightly worse than having to get up an hour earlier due to daylight savings time.

When you want to "shower," you unscrew the cap, and a pathetic drizzle of cold water (heated by the sun, my ass) dribbles down upon you. It sort of feels like being peed on, though at least that would be warm. Thankfully, these were temporary facilities, and my in-laws built a studio apartment, complete with working, flushing toilet. My in-laws are tiny people and therefore do not require much space. After a few years, they added a casita, or one-room guesthouse, on their property. After a few *more* years, they realized all of their children had families of their own and had therefore outgrown the guesthouse, so they added a second bedroom to it. The end result is that the guesthouse is far bigger than the living space they've allotted themselves, but they were willing to do this if it meant they'd get to spend more time with their grandchildren.

I've never lived in Alaska, but Boise can get pretty miserable in the wintertime. Unless you ski, there's really no reason to stay in Boise throughout the winter if you have the choice to do otherwise. I've never understood the "summer sucks" bumper stickers. It's sort of like saying, "I hate sunshine and barbeques and butterflies, and I'd much prefer to scrape ice off my windshield and slip and fall and break my ass every time I walk to my car."

Born and raised in Alaska, my husband inherited the Alaskan cold allergy. The year before, we'd left Boise for the month of February, but in the coming year, Mike wanted to leave for the entire winter, so we booked tickets to Mexico for December 1 through February 28. We enrolled our kids in an English-speaking Montessori school in Mexico for that time and made arrangements to continue working. We even rented out our home in Boise to help offset the mortgage.

"You don't have any problem with strangers living in your house?" Sandi asked.

"It's just a house."

"But they'll be using your stuff."

"It's just stuff."

"And having sex in your bed."

"Hey, you give me five grand, and you can have sex in my bed, too."

"That kind of makes you sound like a whore," she said.

"No," I corrected. "That makes me the pimp. You're the whore."

She nodded as if this all made perfect sense. "How the hell did you get someone to rent your house in Idaho for December, January, and February?" she asked.

"They're moving here," I explained. "From *Alaska.*"

The renters were relocating and needed a home for their family of four while they went through the house-hunting process. This particular family had been living in Fairbanks, so to them, Boise in the wintertime felt like a mild spring.

It's not that I haven't tried to like winter. It's just that it's so... *cold.* And I did try skiing once. It only took me seven years of living within thirty minutes of a ski slope to give it a go. I went one day with Sandi and her husband, Matt. I hadn't gone earlier because that would have meant going with Mike and having him teach me. The absolute worst way to learn anything requiring physical agility is to learn from your spouse. This is a surefire way to get into a massive fight and end up ruining your sex life for the subsequent week because you're so mad at each other. But Sandi and Matt were going up for the day and offered to take me. When the opportunity was presented to me, I told Mike I was thinking of joining them at Bogus Basin, Boise's ski slope. He responded instantly with: "I don't think that's a good idea."

"You don't think it's a good idea for me to try skiing for the first time in my life?"

"It's a bad idea."

"Why is it a bad idea? Because you can't go?"

"No. It's really hard, and I just don't think you'll like it."

"How can you possibly know whether or not I'm going to like skiing?"

"Well, *I* don't really like it."

"But that has nothing to do with me," I reasoned. I could tell that if the conversation headed along its current track, we would be going to bed that evening with nothing but tension between the sheets. I hoped we could get past the issue and instead burn some calories with making up, but that didn't mean I was through speaking my mind. "I have never been skiing in my life, and I have the opportunity to go, and I want to, and you don't want me to. Please explain this to me, because this is exactly why I don't want to bring things like this up with you. I think it's better if I just go instead of saying anything about it, because I know that the second I mention something like this, you're going to shoot down the idea."

"That's not true!" he protested.

"Then tell me why I shouldn't go."

"You might get hurt. It's expensive. There are a million reasons not to go."

"You don't want me to go without you—is that it?"

"No, that's not it. I think I'm just afraid you'll... *like* it."

"Wait... you don't want me to go skiing for fear that I might really enjoy myself?" I thought about this. "It turns out that our relationship is far more screwed up than I knew."

"No, it's not that," he said. "Of course I want you to enjoy yourself. Go skiing, have a good time. I'm sorry. I think I was just afraid you would fall in love with it and want to do it all the time. It's so expensive, and I don't really like it, so I just don't want it to become your new *thing*."

"Here's what's going to happen," I said. "I'm going to go skiing, and I'm going to have a great time. But we both know that I don't like being cold and that I have horrific balance, so I don't really think there's any danger of it becoming my new thing. Besides, I don't want a new thing. I want fewer things. I'm not looking for a new thing."

"Okay," he said. "Seriously, have a good time. And don't break anything."

"I'll try not to."

I bought my ski pass, which seemed positively exorbitant to me as a non-skier. Paying fifty dollars for a day pass would be great if I was actually going to spend a full day there. But really, a "day" on the slopes for me would turn out to be more like two and a half hours, two hours of which would likely be spent in the lodge drinking cocktails. I was thankful at least that we weren't going to someplace really expensive in the realm of skiing, like some over-the-top fancy ski resort where movie stars hang out and you can get your Botox injections in between ski runs.

Matt and Sandi treated me with kid gloves and gave me a basic lesson. Whenever I looked at them, their expressions seemed to be a mix of pity, bewilderment, restrained mirth, and a strong desire not to return to Boise at the end of the day and inform Mike that they'd broken his wife.

I'd thought that it would be physically demanding to get going, which is the case in most sports. It takes effort to move when you run or bike or swim. So I was shocked to learn that with skiing, the opposite is true. Moving is *too* easy. It's slowing down and stopping that will exhaust you, not the other way around.

In the course of the afternoon, I went down the bunny slope half a dozen times. The first time, I fell hard and fast and often, and I can see now why it's so easy to break a bone in this activity. When people talked about hitting the slopes, I didn't know they meant hitting the slopes with your face, which is what I did. I hit the slope face first and then used my face as an anchor in the snow. In a facedown position, my head became a pivot, by which my body spun around in circles. The facial pivot might seem like a rookie move, but without being firmly embedded face down in the snow, I'm convinced that my body would have slid right off the mountain.

"I'm okay!" I screamed to Matt and Sandi when I came to a stop and dislodged my head. I would repeat this phrase often.

Attempting to stand made me feel that I was missing a few joints. My body simply did not possess the capacity to move at an angle that would allow me to once again reach an upright position. Did one need to be double jointed to participate in this sport? And how long do you try unsuccessfully to stand before you look to your fellow skiers and cry for help?

The ski lift was by far the most terrifying part of it all. Every now and then, I have a fear not that I will inexplicably fall to my death, but that I will inexplicably cause my own death. It's as if I'm afraid my body will one day decide to betray me and force me to commit suicide even though I have no intention of doing so. I've never heard anyone else voice this fear, but I surely can't be the only one.

Once I'd convinced them I was proficient enough, which I accomplished by demonstrating my ability to stand, as well as repeated employment of my now-patented facial pivot technique, Sandi and Matt left me to handle the bunny slope on my own. As soon as they did this, I made one more round of the bunny slope before sneaking off to the lodge for a drink. Skiing was fun, but only if you can at one point say, "Okay, I did that without breaking my leg, so now it's time to sit and have a drink." At the bar, I found that I was sitting and drinking with all the people who had injured themselves and were waiting for the rest of their group. That might make me sound like a bit of a loser, but I think I was the smart one. The purpose of skiing seems to be to do it until you are severely injured, at which time you are permitted to adjourn to the bar. All I did was manage to skip the injury, which seems by far the more intelligent option.

Matt and Sandi ended up bickering at each other because Matt didn't ski *with* Sandi. While she thought at one point they would go down one of the slopes together, he pretty much did his own thing, and Sandi felt neglected. In all fairness, it's not as if you can ski while making out or holding hands or really even having a half-decent conversation. Their spat reinforced to me that things like skiing are best undertaken in the absence of one's spouse.

* * *

Mexico represented not just an escape of winter, but also the opportunity to get away from certain aspects of American kid culture that I struggle with, including my greatest nemesis: Chuck E. Cheese. I detest this oversized rodent who entices my children, only to teach them that *funner* is a word. Mr. Cheese's establishment is lamentably close to our home in Boise, and we pass by it often. I managed to get through four years of parenting without going there, but there came a time when it was no longer avoidable. My children deconstructed all of the lies I'd told to keep us out (witches who eat small children live there, et cetera). After that, I instituted a reward chart. A visit to Chuck. E. Cheese was the highest reward, and I figured there was no way my girls could achieve the necessary number of magnetic stars, via good behavior, to reach that reward. Never underestimate the power of small children focused on obtaining something you clearly don't want them to have.

I've learned valuable strategies over time, having had to go there on a handful of occasions. For instance, the timing of a visit to Chuck E. Cheese is key, and I highly recommend right when they open on Sunday mornings, when everyone else is at church. By the time the masses show up, my kids are tired and ready to leave. The problem with the regulars of Chuck E. Cheese lies not with the other children, but with their parents. When I see a two-year-old crying in a corner while his daddy pisses away tokens throwing basketballs through a hoop designed for a seven-year-old, I know that it's time to depart.

I made many rookie mistakes in the beginning, but I've since become a pro. For example, we don't eat there, which we did once, but only because I was so overwhelmed by the flashing lights, ringing bells, and disease-laden carpet that I began throwing my credit card at an employee in the hopes that it would all go away. Instead, he charged me for a pizza.

Tokens must never be given in a free-for-all manner. They are doled out in turns. When it's Emilia's turn, I give her a token, and we must follow her and watch as she uses it. Then it's Ivy's turn, and so on. Sure, this tactic makes me a bit of a Nazi. And yes, I am strangely capable of sucking the fun out of a place where we go to have fun, but *funner* is not a word, and I'm not made of money, damn it. By meting out the tokens, they last, as opposed to just letting the kids have at them, in which case twenty dollars is gone in five minutes. It's the equivalent of slot machines for toddlers. We all know that slot machines are not for toddlers. Slot machines are for the parents of toddlers.

When it's Ivy's turn at Chuck E. Cheese, she takes her token and walks slowly throughout the rides, carefully considering where she'll use it. She'll walk in circles, reveling in the fact that the rest of our group is forced to follow her. She enjoys being the leader and having the attention on her far more than she enjoys any of the rides, and eventually I threaten to decide for her.

Escaping both winter and the funnerness of Chuck E. Cheese sounded great. These things do not exist in Todos Santos, and the prospect of a winter without them was welcome, but there were nagging little annoyances in my brain that pled with me to just stay put in my nice, familiar surroundings where everything is easier. A friend of mine has four children. On a Wednesday, her husband surprised her with a trip for the whole family to Hawaii. They would leave on Friday.

"He couldn't understand why I wasn't thrilled," she told me. "I mean, it's wonderful, and I'm excited, and I'm sure we'll have a great time. On the other hand, part of me thinks, why would I want to go to Hawaii with my husband and four kids? It's like my life—only *harder.*"

"Well, just try and focus on the positive," I said. "And yes, you will all probably have a fantastic time."

"I know." She sighed. "Listen, I've got to run. I have about fifteen loads of laundry to do before we go."

And it's true. Travel with children often seems like my life, only harder. I think it's easy for a lot of men to be disheartened by this or to think of their wives as simply not adventurous, but you can bet your ass those men aren't the ones doing the fifteen loads of laundry. I love travel, but I was daunted by the fact that we'd be traveling for three months. I like to travel to a place for a week and then go back home. At heart, I'm a homebody. After all, if I didn't like my home, I wouldn't live there. If left to my own devices, I could easily become a recluse who survives on Chinese food delivery and watches endless reruns of *COPS* while surrounded by a bevy of stray cats.

When Mike and I first discussed the possibility of going to Mexico for longer than a month, he suggested six months. In the past, when he presented ideas like this, we volleyed our opinions back and forth until I grew weary of the conversation and eventually caved. The discussion ended with me saying, "Whatever you want to do is fine." I did this because I love and trust my husband, and really, whatever he wanted to do was fine. However, that's not to say it didn't come back to bite me in the butt. Just as many times as everything worked out fine, I ended up wishing I'd had a little more fight in me and hadn't given in so easily. So when Mike suggested living in Mexico for six months, I thought about it and decided that three was my max. In hindsight, I wonder if he suggested six knowing that if he did so, I'd at least agree to three. In any case, we decided on three months away. Next time, I'll agree to six just to mess with him and see what he says. Or maybe that's all part of his evil plan.

Along with all of the obvious positives about living in Mexico, I tried to remind myself that the part of it that would be uncomfortable was also a positive. *Get out of your comfort zone! It's good for you.* But I don't actually believe these things because really, what's better than comfort? And as far as the "it's good for you" argument, I'm not buying it. Broken bones are uncomfortable, but that doesn't mean they're good for you. It's along the same lines of thinking as *that which does not kill you makes you stronger,* which is just something that drill sergeants came up with to keep their recruits from going AWOL. But people I admire talk all the time about how it's good to get out of your comfort zone. They say this from the comfort of their plush La-Z-Boy with a cocktail in hand, but there must be an inkling of truth to it.

It takes some preparation getting ready to leave the country for three months. You have to make arrangements for your mail, your house, your cars, and all of the other stuff that comprises daily life. And if you rent your house out to someone else, you have to make it a little more neutral. You also have to leave those people with some closet space. I went about cleaning out my closet to make room for our renters and thought that instead of donating my clothes, maybe I'd try taking them into a used-clothing shop in exchange for store credit. I dropped off a bin of clothes at Plato's Closet, and the young girl who worked there told me they'd call me to let me know how much store credit I'd get. They never called. I forgot about it for a day or two and then called them.

"Oh yeah," said a bored teen on the other end of the line. "We still have your clothes here. You can have them back if you want. We can't take any of them."

"What do you mean you can't take any of them?" This was perplexing. I hadn't dropped off any clothes with stains or tears, and the shoes were all pretty sturdy. I imagined their inventory was just too large. Maybe they'd want me to bring them back in a month or so.

"You might want to try more of a *mature* women's clothing shop. We can't take any of these."

"What?" I couldn't believe the bitch had the audacity to call me mature.

"Yeah, we only take designer jeans, and a lot of the stuff you have is like Eddie Bauer type stuff, so I'd try maybe a mature women's consignment store." There she was with that *mature* woman thing again. I wanted to reach through the phone and slap the gum right out of her mouth. "So, if you want to come pick them up, I can write down a few *mature* women's shops for you, or we can just donate them."

"If you say the word *mature* one more time, I'm going to freak out."

"If I say... *mature?*"

"Fine, donate them!" I slammed down the phone and never again returned to Plato's Closet, though I still contend that I'm not too mature to do so.

Prepping the house also meant putting a lot of our knick-knacks and family photos in big plastic bins. I didn't want someone else to have to deal with our clutter. And just in case they burned the house down, I decided to get a safety deposit box at the bank, where I kept our extra checks and our wills. As I placed the wills into the safety deposit box, I realized that I was officially mature and cursed both Plato and the closet he came out of.

The last time we'd gone to Mexico, it was for just a month, so we let Virgil housesit. When we talked about leaving for three months, all of the neighbors asked if Virgil would once again be housesitting. I always answered that I wasn't opposed to the idea, and they'd purse their lips and let out a troubled "Hmmm." There were reports of a lot of people in our house. I was also told by other relatives who stopped in to check on the house that it was a disaster.

"Oh my god," Sandi warned. "I saw the place last time. Believe me, you do not want him to housesit again."

"It looked fine by the time we got back," I said.

"I know, and I even lied to him about when you were coming back to make sure he had everything cleaned up in time."

"Good thinking," I said.

They were concerned because they know that I'm a neat freak and didn't want me to suffer a heart attack upon our return. But Virgil cleared out the masses and left the home in good condition. There were a few traces of neglect, like the one plant I'd asked him to water. It was drooping and near death but sopping wet. There were also water stains on the wall behind it, as if two minutes before we came in he remembered he was supposed to have been watering the plant in the weeks prior, ran to the kitchen for some sort of receptacle, and hurled water at the plant. There was also a stain of some sort of liquid that had been splashed against another wall. Either Virgil had an indoor water balloon fight, someone was sloshed and splattered a beverage all over the wall, or perhaps both. But really, I'm not concerned with these things. Virgil cleaned up before we came home, and the house was still standing. However, if my choice is between that or getting five grand from someone who wants to rent my house, I'm afraid I'm going to go for the five grand. It seems like the mature decision.

* * *

CHAPTER TEN

Mommy Had a Little Flask

I woke with a start from a nightmare. Everywhere I went, young, skinny, beautiful, hot singers from Nashville called me a mature woman. I tried to tell them to shut the fuck up, but my teeth fell out. An Eddie Bauer-clad Kevin Spacey put a hand on my shoulder and gently told me that it was time to look into dentures and that he'd take me to a dentist, right after Keyser Söze had his way with a young, skinny, beautiful, hot singer from Nashville. Oh, the horror.

But Mike and I were destined for a night out on the town that evening, so I shook it off. The babysitter arrived, and we headed out for drinks. While we walked downtown, we passed a lot of young people with raging hormones. Girls with barely any clothes on, boys doing pull-ups on trees to catch the eye of a girl with barely any clothes on. As we walked down the sidewalk in a nice part of town, a car full of boys drove by, and one of them leaned out of the window and shouted at Mike, "Hey, buddy, your girlfriend's a slut!" Mike clucked his tongue, shook his head in disapproval, and quietly muttered something about ripping the guy's face off. But I took the comment as flattery. At least he hadn't called me mature.

We went to a bar, sat outside, and ordered drinks. The town seemed full of twenty-year-olds. After our drinks arrived, two girls at a table next to us pulled their table up to ours.

"I'm sorry to interrupt," one of them slurred. "Can we join you?"

"Sure," I said, noting that she was drinking sangria and would have a wicked hangover the next day.

"Are you guys married?" she asked.

"We are," I answered.

"Thirteen years," added Mike.

"Oh my god, that's *so crazy*," Sangria said. "And you obviously still like each other." She looked at her friend then. "What's wrong with us?"

"I don't know," said Friend.

"Our boyfriends are lame," said Sangria. "They could've come out with us, but they wanted to stay home and play video games." Okay, she didn't actually say "video games," because that's what my generation says. She named the actual game, which I can't remember now, but it was something along the lines of "Big Bad Characters with Guns."

"Dump them," said Mike.

"And they hardly ever want to have sex," said Sangria.

"Yeah, dump them," I agreed.

"I just don't get it," continued Sangria. "I mean, okay, I'm chubby, but whatever. But look at her." She gestured to Friend. "She's totally hot, and her boyfriend is so *blah* about sex."

"Except when we travel," said Friend. "We travel great together. When we travel, we have sex all the time."

"Porn," said Mike.

"What?" asked Friend.

"He's jerking off to porn all the time. When you travel, he doesn't have it with him, so you guys have lots of sex, but at home, he's spent from all the porn."

Friend and Sangria looked at each other and nodded, and I knew Mike had just solved a mystery for them. I was shocked at how quickly we'd entered into a therapy session with these two strangers, but they were far more likable than the other drunks floating about town.

"Do you guys have kids?" asked Sangria.

"We do," I answered. "A three-year-old and a five-year-old."

"Oh my god, that's crazy. I hate kids." She didn't mean this maliciously. She was just drunk and blurting out basically the same way I felt about kids when I was her age. "We both have dogs, though, and we love our dogs." She got out her phone and showed me pictures of her dogs.

"Huh," I said. "I hate dogs."

"You what? How can you hate dogs! No one hates dogs! I can't believe you just said that right after I showed you a picture of my baby."

"Actually, you showed me a picture of your *dog*. You don't have a baby. And I said it right after you learned I have children and told me that you hate them."

She looked thoughtful for a moment and then nodded. "Touché."

Going out was fun, but the bulk of our interactions did little to assuage the nagging feeling that I was suddenly older than the rest of the world and definitely not hip.

We had a cocktail party coming up, and I thought perhaps

it would be more my style. It's not that I'm old, I reasoned, and it's certainly not that I'm mature, it's just that I have finer tastes and need a classier crowd. *This cocktail party will be perfect. I'll fit right in.* But then I learned more about it and about our hosts. They were beautiful and rich, as in really beautiful and really rich. This shouldn't have been intimidating, but for some reason it was. I was determined to wear an actual cocktail dress, something that would make me fit in with all of the beautiful, rich people with whom we'd be mingling. I even made an appointment to have my hair done. The dress I wanted to wear was a decade old but still fit as long as I didn't breathe. I braved the mall to buy my first "body shaper," which is something I should have purchased years ago. Anyone who complains about the cost of a good body shaper should get an estimate for liposuction. A body shaper is far less expensive and invasive. Of course, getting off your ass and running for an hour is free.

The day of the cocktail party, I went to see my hairdresser. She works at a salon where all of the employees are shockingly and annoyingly beautiful, including the stunning husband and wife team that owns the business. Whenever I run into them, I expect them to be assholes, because I want exceptionally beautiful people to have a fatal flaw, but they don't. The wife periodically competes in the amateur body-building scene. She's managed to do this without slowly turning into a man, meaning that she's maintained her gorgeous femininity and does not have veins threatening to burst from her skin.

"Hey, Amanda, how are you?" she said as I walked in. "Here to see Georgia?"

"I am," I replied. "How are you?"

"Awesome."

"Are you training for a competition right now? You look crazy buff." I tried not to be too creepy in surveying her perfectly sculpted arms.

"Yes. I had *tilapia* for breakfast. Two ounces of tilapia with nothing on it." She had a smile that spoke of little remaining sanity.

"I'm sorry."

"That's okay. It's almost over. Can I get you anything to drink? Would you like a water?"

"I'd love a..." I really wanted a diet Coke. I don't usually drink it, but I knew they had it, and it sounded perfect. "I'll have a..."

"A water?"

"Sure, I'll have a water." Asking for a soda from someone training for a body-building competition feels like sending pictures of the Chuck-A-Rama buffet to starving kids in Africa. It's just cruel.

"Here you go. And I think Georgia is just about ready for you."

"Thanks," I said. "And good luck."

I found Georgia and immediately whispered into her ear: "Can you get your hands on a diet Coke for me?"

"Let me guess," she whispered back. "You didn't feel comfortable asking at the front desk?"

"She had two ounces of *tilapia* for breakfast."

"I know," said Georgia. "We all hide from her when we eat lunch."

Georgia snuck me a soda, which I kept hidden under my drape, save for the hurried and occasional sip.

"What are we doing today?" Georgia asked.

"Make me pretty."

"What's the occasion?"

"A rich-people party," I said. "They even have drivers to take people and their vehicles home."

"Cool!"

"Sort of, but that's almost too much of a license to get drunk, which I'm really good at, so I think maybe I should be a designated driver so I don't get drunk and make a fool of myself in front of all the rich people."

"I wouldn't worry about it," she said. "Rich people get way more drunk than other people. They get crazy drunk, and they always start smashing plates and glasses and shit. Mark my words. Someone will purposefully smash a plate by the end of the evening."

"Huh. I'll let you know." Georgia put fifty thousand bobby pins in my hair to get it in some sort of chignon, whatever that may be. It's also a word I do not dare pronounce, for fear of saying it wrong. Just like my refusal to say khaki for a decade, because it always sounded like I was trying to say the word cock while hopped up on Novocain. Regardless of how my hairstyle should be pronounced, it looked awesome.

"Do you want me to do your makeup, too?"

I planned on doing my own makeup, but when someone offers to do something for me, I have little trouble agreeing, so after my hair was in place and sufficiently shellacked, she applied my makeup.

"I'm going to clean up your eyebrows," she said.

"What?" Surely she wasn't talking about plucking my eyebrows; my eyebrows were perfect. Maybe "clean up" meant something else. Were my eyebrows dirty? Do people cleanse their eyebrows regularly like washing their hands, and I just didn't know about it? She approached me with a pair of tweezers, and I realized that by cleaning up, she *did* mean plucking. Apparently, she felt my eyebrows needed some pruning.

"Have you *looked* at my eyebrows?" I asked. "They've never been plucked before. They're virgin."

"Why haven't you ever plucked them before? Is it against your religion or something?"

"They've never been plucked because they've never *needed* to be plucked. Seriously, look at them. They're by far my best feature."

She took a good, close look and then frowned. "Yeah, they need some cleaning up. Hold this." She handed me a mirror. "Watch." She plucked my eyebrows. I'd expected something excruciating, but it didn't hurt that bad. Still, I was skeptical of what the results would bring. I had perfect brows; that was my claim to fame. She continued a pluck here and there and— *voila!* It was a whole new me. I was shocked at the difference and cursed myself for having spent my life thus far walking around looking like a Neanderthal. What else was I missing out on? Maybe I should look into lash extensions after all. No, I warned myself. Don't do anything rash. Or anything that may cause a rash.

With my hair back in a style uncharacteristically elegant for me and my freshly manicured brows, a new flaw showed in startling light. My cheeks looked like I was ready for a cameo in a *Planet of the Apes* movie. I had peach fuzz galore, and with my hair back, it was more than evident.

"I should probably do something about all of this hair on my face," I said.

I was hoping Georgia would say, "What are you talking about? I don't see any hair," or "You're imagining the rug lining your jowls, because I can't see a thing."

But Georgia is painfully honest and instead responded with, "I'm sure it will be dark at the party." I thanked her for her skills in making me look better than I actually do and went home to get dressed.

With body shaper firmly in place, I donned my beautiful cocktail dress and admired myself in the mirror. I looked great, save for the fur on my face. I knew better than to take a razor to it. I didn't want to end up managing a persistent stubble for the rest of my life. Instead, I took the wiser path and began ripping the little bastards off my face with my fingers, though I resolved the next day to buy some sort of product that would aid in the correct way for a woman to remove hair from her face.

We drove far up into the foothills over Boise to a beautiful home. In the foothills, it gets windy, and it was kind of cold to begin with. I was further dismayed to see that the bulk of the party took place outside on a deck with a view of Boise. Outdoor heaters were set up, but I'd have to spend the evening humping one of them if I was going to avoid freezing to death. Also, I appeared to be the only woman wearing an actual cocktail dress. Apparently I missed the cultural shift when "cocktail dress" stopped referring to fancy attire suitable for a fancy cocktail party and started meaning "whatever the fuck you feel like wearing." This was disconcerting, along with the fact that I didn't really know any of the people there. I did my best to appear not cold, to not get completely wasted, and to make polite conversation with the others in attendance. This worked for a little while, until religion came into a conversation I was having with another couple.

Mike was mingling, so he wasn't there to kick me in the shin at the appropriate time. When others casually talk about the teachings of their religion and the religious figures they worship, I feel compelled to casually mention my lack of religion. This never goes well. I instantly see the change in the people I'm speaking with. Whereas they may have been laughing a moment before, when they assumed we were all on the same spiritual page, their faces drop upon learning otherwise, the joy is sucked from their expressions, and while they stay and nod for a moment longer, I can see the seed of hatred forming in their eyes. They no longer want to speak with me or associate with me because I do not believe the things they do. This isn't always a problem. I'm not hostile to other people's religions, and I have many friends of various religions, but those friends respect that I have my own religious choices to make.

Not long after I'd gone public as a heathen, I wrapped things up and decided it was time to leave the party. Mike drove, as we had no need for a set of drivers to see us and our vehicle home safely. On the way home, he asked how everything went.

"I thought it went fine," I said.

"Yeah, me too," he agreed.

"Although, there was one moment when religion came up."

"Oh no. What did you say?"

"Nothing!"

"Come on, what did you say?"

"I didn't say anything horrible. I didn't insult anybody. I just may have casually mentioned that I'm not religious after they casually mentioned that they're Christian."

"Honey!"

"What? I didn't do anything wrong! Why is it okay for others to work their religion into the conversation at a cocktail party and it's not okay for me to mention my lack of religion?"

"Oh, Lord," he said.

"What? Should I have lied? You know I'm a shitty liar."

"No. I'm not asking you to lie about anything. But why can't you just keep quiet? Why does religion have to come up in the first place?"

"*They* brought it up."

"Fine. Let's just move on."

We were quiet for a moment, and I slipped off my torturous heels. "You know how I said I'm a really shitty liar?"

"What now?" He cringed in anticipation of what I might say.

"Well, *I* may have brought up the subject of religion. I'm not sure how, but yes, I think it was actually all my fault."

* * *

The next day, I felt I needed some serious pampering to get over the awkwardness of the previous evening, so naturally I went to the grocery store to buy cream for removing facial hair. Purchasing this gave me the same feeling I get when buying something to cure a yeast infection. Like hemorrhoids or a good fungus, it's not something you want to acknowledge. But I was convinced that this product would make my life better, so I purchased it and hid it among seventy-five other items that I didn't need. After careful consideration, I chose a checkout line worked by an older woman who I was pretty sure wouldn't pass judgment on my purchase. When she finished up with the person in line before me, she said, "Just a moment." Apparently her shift was at its end, and Josh, who looked to be about fourteen, took over.

I didn't like Josh. He looked insolent and condescending, and I remembered him from previous trips to the store as the kid who bagged my groceries with cans on top of bread and sushi upside down. Part of the allure of sushi is the presentation. Sushi is beautiful as well as delicious. When I get home and it's a big mish-mashed pile of rice and wasabi all crushed to one side, I feel like crying.

Josh took the reins, and there was no way of getting out of it because I had all seventy-six items already up on the conveyor belt. As usual, he placed a loaf of bread into a bag and then covered it with canned goods. Is bagging groceries really that hard? He worked mindlessly, as if he couldn't care less about the things that I was buying. That is, until the facial Nair came up. Instead of just swiping it over the sensor as he had with everything else I'd purchased, he actually stopped and held the box up to study it, to read the front of it and figure out exactly what this little product was supposed to do for me. Then he lowered the box, scanned it, and placed it into its own little bag, like how you'd treat a greeting card or something delicate like a wine glass. It was as if he singled out the hair remover, acknowledging to me that he knew this was what I'd come for. When he gave me my total and I swiped my card, I swear he leaned in and squinted at me, studying my face. At that moment, I wished that grocery store clerks worked for tips, so that I could fail to give him one. I thought of complaining, but what sort of recourse did I have? Sure, I could complain to the manager, but what would I say? "Josh looked too long at my facial hair remover and then at my face to see if I needed it." That would only further highlight my problem and cause the manager to assess my jowls with the same condescending scrutiny. I cursed him in my mind and took my leave.

At home, I carefully read the directions and then smeared some of the cream over the peach fuzz on my jaw. I waited a few minutes as directed and then rinsed it off. As if by magic, my face was transformed from *Planet of the Apes* to *Planet of People without Excessive Hair on Their Faces*. It was wonderful, smooth and perfect.

"This stuff is awesome," I said to myself. I took a picture of the product with my phone and sent a text to Sandi.

Me: This stuff is great.
Sandi: Where do you have hair on your face?
Me: Peach fuzz on the jawline, but this stuff does the trick.

But then I looked closer and saw a very distinct line from where I'd had the cream. *Oh dear,* I thought, *I'd better do this again.* I had to cover more of my face so that it wasn't so obvious that some parts of my face had hair and some did not. After the second time around, I felt I'd done a pretty good job. But then I used a hand mirror to look at the sides and back of my neck, and there was the same problem: a distinct line between where the natural hairs that cover my skin were and where they were not.

Me: I wish you were here to tell me if I'm patchy or not. In the future, don't let me do this without another female present.

Sandi: Noted.

I applied the cream about five different times until I was satisfied that there weren't any indicative lines. I sent Sandi another text on the matter.

Me: Skin now burning. This could be bad.

Sandi: You can no longer make fun of me for burning my face off.

Me: Noted.

* * *

Between our downtown adventure and the rich people party, I decided that simply taking a "traveler" to the park was more my speed. That weekend when the kids woke up, I brewed a pot of coffee and spiked a travel mug with Bailey's. As I returned the Bailey's to its home, Emilia said, "Mom, what's that silver thing?" She pointed to a glint inside the liquor cabinet.

"That's called a flask," I said.

"Can I use it?" she asked.

"No, a flask is a special container for special drinks."

"Are you going to use it?"

"No. I'm just going to take my coffee cup." The flask in question has never been used, because I'm not that hardcore. It was a gift, and it waits in the liquor cabinet in case I ever become that hardcore.

Emilia had no further questions on the matter, and she, Ivy, and I walked down to our local park. We found it deserted, save for one little girl who looked to be about six years old. The three girls immediately struck up a friendship. The new girl had sandals that repeatedly fell off; eventually she gave up and went barefoot. My girls then took off their socks and shoes.

"No, girls. Please keep your socks and shoes on."

"But *she* has no socks and shoes," Emilia protested.

"Yes, but this is bark, and I don't want to spend the afternoon pulling splinters out of your feet. That's why we wore socks and shoes, so just worry about yourself and put your socks and shoes back on." Then I addressed my daughters' new friend. "What's your name?"

"Sadie."

"Are your parents here, Sadie? Who are you with?"

"My grandma's over there." She pointed across the field to where a small group was gathered at a picnic table. It looked like a birthday celebration.

"Okay," I said and silently judged Grandma for not bringing her granddaughter with appropriate footwear, as well as for failing to supervise the child. Though I'm sure Grandma would have equally judged me for spiking my coffee. I helped Sadie a few different times, pulling splinters out of her feet, putting her sandals on and then taking them off again a moment later, and picking her up when she couldn't reach the water fountain. Then Grandma shifted her fat ass and hollered over that it was time for Sadie to come back to the picnic table. *Just a minute,* I thought, *Sadie's busy receiving basic parental care from a complete stranger while you finish that bag of chili-dog-flavored Doritos. No, really, don't get up.* Sadie waved a quick goodbye and ran to Grandma, who appeared to scowl at me for helping her granddaughter. Emilia, Ivy, and I decided it was time to return home. On our way, we passed by the picnic table. Grandma scowled at me again. Emilia capped off the interaction perfectly by speaking directly to Grandma while pointing to my coffee cup. "My mommy just has coffee," she stated. "She's not using the flask today."

* * *

CHAPTER ELEVEN

Red Light, Green Dot

By the time the date had come for us to embark on our three months in Mexico, we were shockingly ready. I packed my Nair, to which I had grown addicted, we turned the keys to our home over to our renters, who seemed like nice people with no intention of setting up a meth lab in our basement, and spent the night before our early morning flight in a hotel downtown. We did this partly because we knew that getting to the airport on time would be much easier if we were just packing up and leaving a hotel room as opposed to packing up and leaving from home. But the main reason we spent the night prior in a hotel room was that we had a voucher for a free night's stay. We let the kids jump on the beds, watch an obnoxious tween sitcom, and have their last bath for a while. Not that we eschewed bathing or hygiene while south of the border, but most homes in Todos Santos, including my in-laws', only have showers. They have *real* showers, as opposed to the I-hate-the-fucking-sun-shower showers, but still, no bathtubs. The kids would have to toughen up and learn to shower.

The next morning, we checked out, took a shuttle to the Boise Airport, and went through security without a hitch. We settled in a small play area with a Lego table for a while before boarding our plane to LAX. I like early morning flights because it's nice to get a head start on a long day of travel, to arrive at our destination before the sun has set and while there's still time to get the children sufficiently settled. I don't like early morning flights because it's not acceptable to order a drink on a plane at 8 a.m. And I felt a drink would have been entirely appropriate since we were heading to my least favorite airport. I can't stand LAX. It is typically a disaster, and I was especially nervous because we had a layover of only thirty minutes. I imagined us missing our plane and having to spend a night there.

There was no need for apprehension about making our tight connection; we'd forgotten that all planes departing LAX fail to do so on time. We lingered around the terminal for a while, shuffling back and forth between three different gates as our departure gate continued to change. I'm sure the pilots don't keep reparking the planes at different gates, or changing their minds as to where they'll eventually stop a plane, so why is it that a departure gate can change three different times in fifteen minutes? Or is this just the terminal staff's way of screwing with us, distracting us from the fact that the plane is taking off an hour after it's supposed to? Eventually we did leave LAX, and by that time it seemed perfectly reasonable to drink on the plane, so I enjoyed a bloody Mary while Emilia and I attempted to do the crossword puzzle in the inflight magazine. It was my job to figure out the answers and her job to write the letters in the tiny boxes.

Travel with children ages three and five is a walk in the park compared to flying with an infant who wants to be breastfed and then craps so much that a mere diaper cannot restrain the flood of poop that somehow migrates up the back to emerge at the top of the onesie. This is followed by dirty looks from childless passengers, angry that your daughter has stunk up the plane, and pity from other parents as you try to change her diaper and clothing while de-pooping her along the way. This was our first trip without diapers, diaper bags, strollers, and the hundreds of amenities that make babies so maddeningly high-maintenance.

Emilia and I eventually gave up on the crossword, coming to the sad conclusion that Mommy is just not that smart and perhaps needs to brush up on her knowledge of Roman gods and the geography of India.

"Mom, how long are we going to be in Mexico?" Emilia asked.

"We'll be there for three months."

"Is three months a lot?"

"Sort of. We'll be there ninety days."

"Ninety days?" Her eyes grew wide. "How many big sleeps is that?"

In our family, a big sleep is not a reference to death or a Raymond Chandler novel, but rather to sleeping at nighttime, as opposed to the little sleeps of napping during the day.

"Ninety days is the same as ninety sleeps," I explained.

"Wow," she said. "I can't believe we're going for nine whole days! That's a lot!"

I decided to leave it at that.

"Mom?"

"Yes?"

"I'm really going to miss Charlie."

"I know, sweetie. We'll see him when we get back."

Charlie was Emilia's best friend and the boy she had chosen to someday marry. They'd had many play dates during which Emilia suggested they play ball.

"Sure," Charlie would answer, picking up a ball and readying himself for a game of catch.

"Not like that. It's where we dance around like this." She'd then demonstrate by waltzing around the room with an imaginary prince, one whose shoes she hoped Charlie would fill.

"You know, Emilia, you might meet some new friends in Mexico."

"I know, Mom. But I still want to marry Charlie."

With conversations like these, we passed the time until the terrain below us became the distinct water and desert of the Baja peninsula. Whenever we arrive in Mexico and deplane, there's always a sense of frenzy to get into the terminal and to customs. People elbow one another and rudely sprint so as not to be cast to the back of the line. This is ridiculous, but it's hard not to get caught up in the herd mentality. Once we got off the plane, I took charge of Emilia, and Mike took charge of Ivy. I grabbed Emilia by the hand and walked quickly toward the terminal.

Mike hates lines. He freaks out if he has to wait too long. He panics. This happens in traffic, too. So much so that I've offered to take the wheel while stuck in a sea of cars on a six-lane highway, just to avoid the very real danger that he might bolt from the car and run in search of a bridge from which to leap. There's something about being trapped with the inability to move forward that he can't stand. I get overwhelmed by crowds of people, but I like being in lines. Lines have order to them. They imply the presence of a greater system instead of the anarchy of a free-for-all, during which I'd surely be trampled to death. Lines are my friends. But in an effort to be first in line and thereby lessen Mike's panic, I took Emilia's hand, and we went for it. I figured when Mike and Ivy caught up, they could join us at the coveted spot. But then I heard Mike, his voice sharp. "Amanda! Amanda!" I stopped and waited for him and Ivy to reach us. Ivy's face was tear-stained, and her chubby little legs were moving as fast as they could. Dozens of passengers passed us. "Slow down," he said.

"Sorry. I know about your line phobia and was trying to get us a good spot."

"Ivy wants you, and you're running away from us."

For the second leg of the trip, Mike had been with Ivy, and I sat with Emilia. Apparently Ivy had missed me dearly during that flight, and Mike had assured her that she would be reunited with me when we got off the plane, at which time I promptly sprinted as fast as I could away from her.

We made it through customs, waiting in a line that always moves surprisingly fast. The Mexican officials are actually very efficient, but we somehow forget this on every trip. The next task was to retrieve our luggage. My heart always skips a beat until I see that every last piece has arrived, because one of the crappiest travel feelings is when you realize that your luggage is simply not there. But all of our luggage arrived, and we approached the final security step, where one passenger from each party is asked to present their customs form and then press a button. The button is attached to a stoplight with red and green lights. If you get green, you walk on through. If you get red, you get searched.

"When we get to the light," I said to Mike, "I want you to press it."

"Why?"

"Because we're overdue for a red one, and if we get the red one, and I'm the one who pressed the button, I'm going to suffer from an irrational sense of guilt."

"That's ridiculous," he said. "The button is random. If you get red, it's not like you've done anything wrong."

"I know. That's why I said it's an *irrational* sense of guilt. But it's still there, so I'd rather you do it so that I can say it's your fault when we get the red button."

"You're acting like we're smuggling in a suitcase full of cocaine," he said.

"Don't be ridiculous. I only brought half a suitcase full of cocaine."

"Maybe we shouldn't joke about this."

"You're probably right."

But when we approached the stoplight, as is always the case, I was first to arrive, and therefore they told me to press the button. It was green, and instead of blaming myself for a search of our luggage and a delay to our official arrival, I blamed myself for needlessly worrying about a search of our luggage and a delay to our official arrival.

We made our way out into the freedom of the terminal, and there was my father-in-law waiting for us. Emilia and Ivy ran to him with open arms and the cry of "Papa!"

Papa was picking us up at a brand-new terminal at the Cabo Airport where the powers that be, as he found out, had decided not to let anyone park anymore—unless you had proof that you were there to pick someone up. I'm not sure if they wanted him to produce an itinerary, a lock of hair, or a bribe. In any case, having no luck getting past security, Papa parked far away and walked over to the terminal so that he was there when we arrived.

"I have to walk back and get the truck, and I have to show proof that I'm here to pick someone up, so let me take one of the girls with me," he said.

That seemed terribly weird, but Emilia went with Papa, and the rest of us waited at the curb with our mountain of luggage. Papa and Emilia walked to the truck, drove toward the new terminal, and were stopped by security.

"You're the guy that tried to get through here before," one of the guards said.

"We told you to bring proof you're picking someone up," said the other.

"Here's your proof," said Papa, motioning to Emilia.

"Hi, my name's Emilia, and I'm five years old."

"Now let me go get the rest of my family," Papa demanded. They let him through.

As we waited by the curb, Ivy dissolved into a torrent of tears, distraught that Papa had been there to greet us and then had walked away. It had been a long day of travel, and she was tired and feeling repeatedly deserted. Papa and Emilia pulled up, and we strapped the kids into borrowed car seats, loaded the luggage, and began the drive to Todos Santos.

"So, I met this guy who lives in Pescadero, and he's been working on my back," my father-in-law said. "And he's really kind of a garoo."

Mike turned from the front seat to glance at me in the back. I shrugged my shoulders.

Papa continued, "My back's been out of whack for a while, and I know you've always had back problems, so if you want to come with me next time, he might be able to take a look at you."

"That's great," Mike said. "But what did you say he was?"

"Well, he does some chiropractic work but not like a typical chiropractor. I think he's really a garoo at what he does."

"A what?"

"A ga*roo*. You know, like an expert at it."

Mike glanced back at me again, but I still had no clue. Then it hit him. "Dad?" he asked. "Do you mean a *gu*ru?"

"Yeah," said his father. "He's a real ga*roo*."

We arrived in Todos Santos just before sunset, traveled through town, passed the Super Pollo, the playground of rusty, jagged metal, through an arroyo, and over dirt roads to Nana and Papa's. Their property was lush with bougainvillea and various agave and palms. Their apartment sat adjacent to the casita, the two-room house that we would call home for the next three months. We shellacked the children in bug spray before setting them free to explore every inch of their new home. Then, with margaritas in hand, we settled in to watch the sun sink to the ocean.

"Get ready for the flash," said Papa.

"There's no flash," said Mike.

"There is, too! Well, not all the time, but most of the time. I think there's going to be one tonight. Get ready for it. Here it comes."

For years, we were instructed to watch the Todos Santos sunset with a keen eye in hopes of catching the "green flash." For years, we did so and saw nothing while rational, sane adults standing next to us would swear by it. It's like the *Emperor's New Clothes.* You don't see anything but figure you must have blinked at the precise moment of the flash, until eventually you suspect a town-wide conspiracy in which your friends and family are trying to drive you crazy by insisting on the presence of that which does not exist. I concede that if the conditions are right, the last sight of sun takes on a green hue as it disappears behind the water. This is a far cry from a *flash,* from a blinding light that shoots through the sky.

"It's not a flash, Dad. It's a speck. It's a dot. You should start calling it the green dot."

"I don't want to call it the *dot.* There's nothing exciting about a *dot.* It's a flash, and I'm going to call it a flash."

"Dot," asserted Mike.

"Here it comes," said Papa excitedly. "There it was! That was a good one!" He ignored his nay-saying son and turned to me. "Did you see it? Did you see the flash?"

Part of me wanted to say yes just to feed his enthusiasm, but a greater part enjoys being contrary. "Sorry," I said. "Pure dot."

* * *

CHAPTER TWELVE

El Drinko

"Well, you know what they say. You can't always lead a horse to water."

I thought about this for a moment and stared at my father-in-law, wondering if the folly in what he'd just said was going to occur to him, or if I was going to get the opportunity to point it out. I'm torn in these situations, because I so badly want to identify the error. It's like a game, and I have the answer, and I'm dying to blurt it out. On the other hand, my father-in-law's speech is riddled with misused words and phrases, so when I point out *all* of his mistakes, I come across like the incredible nagging bitch that I am. Most of the time, it's simply too much for me to take, and I can't help myself.

"Actually," I said, "you *can* lead a horse to water." He looked at me in confusion. "But you can't make him *drink*."

Realization struck him, and he put a hand to his head in frustration. "You're going to write about this, aren't you?" he asked.

"No, I promise."

He grumbled in blatant distrust and set about his morning routine. His property in Todos Santos is not expansive, but he has managed to turn it into a wondrous place of flowering plants, hidden gardens, and the best of what the native foliage has to offer. Papa's mornings involve taking great care walking around in his uniform of plaid pajama pants and white T-shirt to make sure all of the flowers get the water they need. While he does this, shuffling in slippers and dragging a great hose behind him, he wears the most gigantic headphones I've ever seen. They make me think of an airport, and instead of lugging a hose, I feel he should wield glowing orange batons with which to carefully guide an airplane to its gate. The headphones receive a signal from the television. He turns on the news, dons his headphones, and listens to the politics of the morning while watering his plants. The rest of us inside don't care to listen nearly as much as Papa does, so we turn the volume down on the TV and occasionally glance at the headlines. This does not interfere with the sound Papa gets through the huge headphones as he meanders about. The sight of him in pajamas and with great black circles hugging the sides of his head was initially amusing but quickly became commonplace. If I saw him watering the plants *without* headphones, something would seem distinctly out of place, and my immediate reaction would be to rush to his aid to see what was amiss.

In an effort to placate our children one morning, Nana offered to put a television show on after breakfast. The children cheered at this idea. Nana turned up the volume and changed the channel to *Dora the Explorer*. No matter how I try to escape Dora, she finds me, just like the creepy but strangely attractive, mustachioed ex in *Sleeping with the Enemy*. At the moment when Nana changed the channel, I watched Papa from the window, watering his roses and taming his bougainvillea. He shuddered in shock and surprise as the discussions of partisan politics and tax reform that boomed through his headphones morphed into the overly enthusiastic voice of Dora, proclaiming her love of strawberries and how she looks forward to sharing them with her boot-clad monkey. This was followed by a slump of Papa's shoulders as he silently resigned himself to the commandeering of his television.

Mornings at Nana and Papa's house were a whirlwind of activity, and their constant comings and goings resulted in a tornado of open doors. I entered and exited buildings with lightning speed because of constant paranoia that mosquitos hovered outside, waiting for the opportunity to come in and devour my family. During the times of day when mosquitos were the worst, usually mid-morning and again right at dusk, I became the screen Nazi and stationed myself near the door so that whenever Nana and Papa came and went, I could make sure the screen was properly shut. I tried to do this with some measure of stealth, or to make it look casual, as if I just happened to be walking by and thought I might close the door, because this is just one in a long list of neurotic Type-A behaviors that I know make me "difficult," but which I am nonetheless unable to curb.

Some situations were an easy fix, like the microwave. I've never before met two people who reheat the same cup of coffee twenty times throughout a morning. Personally, I wouldn't use a microwave to reheat a cup of coffee even once. Heating coffee is a one-shot deal; any attempts to reestablish the desired temperature leave the coffee bitter and undrink-able. My in-laws did not feel this way. They would place a forgotten cup of coffee in the microwave and press start. They would then walk away, forgetting about the coffee. Their microwave in Mexico was specifically designed for people who forget what they were doing. After it finished its programed time, it beeped every thirty seconds as a reminder that it had completed its task. It did this until the door was opened. But my in-laws never heard the beep. They became so conditioned to it that it no longer registered. I would open the microwave and set the coffee cup on the counter, just to stop the incessant beeping. The mug would later be found, and Nana or Papa would take a sip, realize the coffee was cold, and put it back in the microwave so that the process could repeat itself. As ridiculous as this cycle was, it didn't bother me. I'll take being beeped at over bitten any day.

When my efforts at Operation: Don't Get Eaten Alive, also known as Shut the Front Door, failed, and Nana became fully aware of my obsession with closed doors, she attempted to assist and encouraged her husband to do the same. Papa then began closing doors, but with such force that they closed and then rebounded. Mike watched my frustration with the situa-tion and approached me delicately. "Honey," he said, handing me a can of bug spray, "you have to pick your battles." I took this to heart, especially since we were moving into their space and robbing Papa of his morning news.

That night and in the middle of a dream, I felt something scurry across my face. There was only a second in between the scurry and the time it took for me to be fully awake and leap-ing out of bed. As I flew from the bed, my hand batted at my face, and I felt a slight crunch in the offender, which I vaulted against the wall. I turned on the light and did a quick shiver of disgust. Mike was immediately awakened by my actions and concerned for me.

"What was it?" he asked.

"It was a roach on my face. I got it off. Help me find it." When you find yourself assaulted by a giant cockroach in the middle of the night, it's not only important to get it off of you, for your sanity, but also to locate it and destroy it. I thought that wherever it landed, it was probably already dead, or at least maimed, recalling the crunch when I'd batted it away. But if I didn't find it, I wouldn't know for sure, and the rest of the night would be spent with crawling skin and paranoia.

Mike turned on a second light and grabbed a flip-flop, our weapon of choice when it comes to giant cockroaches. In the past, people have corrected me, saying that these creatures are in fact Palmetto bugs, but I really don't give a damn because calling them Palmetto bugs doesn't make them cuddly and doesn't fully communicate their creepiness. Thus, I'll stick with cockroach. We crept around the room, Mike with his flip-flop cocked and ready, me cradling my face as if the bug had actually done physical harm.

"There it is," he said. He pointed to the brown beast, still and silent on the floor beside a suitcase. He stalked it and brought the flip-flop down upon it. "I got it!"

"I think it was already dead," I said. "I heard a crunch when I slapped it off of my face." He looked at me as if I'd just slapped him in the face with a flip-flop. "I mean, it might have been alive," I corrected myself. "So thank you." He still looked a bit sullen. "You're my knight in shining flannel."

"Let's just go back to bed," he said.

And so we did, and I should have just let him go on believing that he'd saved me from the villainous roach. But once again, I had to correct everyone and everything around me. I wondered if having a roach crawl across my face in the middle of the night wasn't some sort of cosmic penance for this flaw. But then I quickly dismissed that notion, because having a roach crawl across your face is just plain wrong. Sure, bugs are annoying, but they usually know better than to crawl across a person's face.

Regardless of the fact that we'd located and destroyed the roach, I spent the night in fits and twitches. I gave up the hope of sleep and resigned myself to reading, but even then scratched and swatted at imaginary beasts.

* * *

We quickly settled into a dinner routine in Todos Santos of feeding the girls and then resetting the table for the adults. Our casita didn't have a kitchen, so everyone was dependent on Nana and Papa's studio for meals.

While Emilia and Ivy worked diligently one night on coloring books that depicted Spanish-speaking Pixar characters, the four adults sat down to dinner. Somehow, the dinner conversation covered my first ever attempt at smoking pot. At the age of thirty. When I'd regrettably crapped my pants.

"Why are we talking about this?" I asked.

"Well, we've all had the fear of the fart," Nana chimed in.

"The fear of the *fart?*" Mike said incredulously. Not only was this a phrase he was unfamiliar with, but also not one he'd expected to hear from his mother.

"Sure, we've all been there," she said.

"You had a story about that, didn't you?" I asked. This was less than desirable dinner conversation, but if it was going to proceed, I wanted someone else to be the main character. "Something about white pants in a Home Depot?"

"Al Roker did it in the White House," added my father-in-law.

"Till the day I die, I won't forget it," said Nana, ignoring Al Roker and reliving whatever had happened in white pants in a Home Depot. "And to this day, I still won't buy orange juice on the street." I didn't ask for further details.

Something caught my peripheral vision then, and I looked to see a dog creeping slowly along the patio outside. It was not Nana and Papa's little white dog, Sitka. This was a bigger dog with a long face and long fur of white and brown. My father-in-law shot up from his chair and began matching the dog's movements, creeping slowly toward the door as if he wanted to sneak up on the dog. Then he opened the sliding glass door and let out a monstrous roar, running after the dog with his arms raised high in the air. It was the universally understood posture of "I'm going to get you."

When he came back inside, Mike and I were trying not to laugh and looking at him for some sort of explanation.

"You ever see a dog crap his pants?" He grinned, indicating that he'd sufficiently frightened off the invading canine. Unfortunately, he said this within earshot of the girls.

"Dogs don't wear pants," said Emilia.

"What's crap?" asked Ivy.

"Oh, what pretty pictures," said Papa, moving away from the crap question. Emilia and Ivy resumed coloring, and Papa returned to the table. "That's Robbie," he explained. "He pisses on everything and eats Sitka's food."

Robbie, it turned out, belonged to one of the neighbors but, like many neighborhood dogs, was permitted to roam free and visit with the community. Nana and Papa's dog, Sitka, was permitted the same freedom. But Robbie was territorial and liked to pee on furniture.

"Does anyone else think it's ironic that this dog that drives you crazy and pees on everything is named Robbie?" I asked. Long before he changed his name to Virgil (because who wouldn't want to change their name to Virgil?), my brother-in-law was Robbie.

My father-in-law sighed as if just the thought of Virgil as a child made him tired.

The next day, I visited with some of the neighbors, Tim and Melissa, and saw the offending Robbie.

"Is this your dog?" I asked.

"No," said Melissa, "but he likes to come and visit. He's a good dog."

"He's not real popular at our place," I said. "He pees on the furniture."

"Yes, I've caught him doing that over here as well. Sitka does it too, though."

"Sitka pees on your furniture?"

"Yes," she confirmed.

Two nights later, Robbie again crept along the patio and silently made his way toward an outdoor rocking chair from which my father-in-law likes to watch the sunset.

"Your friend is back," I told him.

He again took on the persona of a large and loud monster from the old Scooby-Doo cartoons and with raised arms lumbered after the dog, bellowing. When he came back inside, Mike said, "You know, Dad, maybe he wouldn't piss on things if you weren't so mean to him."

"What are you talking about? I know he's a good dog. I'm nice to him."

"I've never seen you be nice to that dog," said Mike.

"Well, he's on my shit list," he conceded. "He pees on my chair, and he eats Sitka's food."

"I get the part about not wanting a dog to pee on your chair," I interjected, "but if you leave dog food out, a dog will eat it."

My father-in-law grunted in response. He has two reactions when someone says something he doesn't want to hear. The first is to play the deaf card and simply pretend you're not there. Sometimes he really is deaf, but other times I suspect he's exercising what he views as his right to selective hearing. The other response to something he doesn't like is a grunt. It's a caveman-like, guttural noise.

I decided to push my luck. "Did you know that Sitka pisses on other people's furniture? I was talking to Melissa the other day, and she says Sitka pees on their chairs."

"And that's okay," he said.

"What?" Mike said.

"Well, Sitka only does it because Robbie does it."

Mike and I rolled our eyes but also realized that there was little left to debate. My father-in-law was as blind to the faults of his dog as any parent is likely to be to the shortcomings of their own child. I've seen parents with hellions talk about the virtues of their little angels and wonder what faults and manipulations my own children exhibit that I willfully deny.

* * *

Over the first two weeks of life in Mexico, we adjusted to a daily routine of work and school during the days and an occasional outing in the evening, sometimes to a local turtle sanctuary or taking Emilia and Ivy into town for ice cream. It was immediately apparent that having Nana along when needing to communicate with the locals was a good idea. This does not mean that Nana speaks Spanish, but rather that the rest of us don't, and Nana has at least made the effort over the years to improve her Spanish, one *poquito* word at a time. When they first began living in Mexico, Nana's attempts at Spanish were so horrific that they became legendary. She's come a long way from flanking every noun with el- and -o, no longer ordering el drink-o or going to el store-o.

Nana, Papa, the girls, and I decided to take a full Saturday and travel into Cabo. Friends of the family own a condo in the oldest condo resort in Cabo, and they invited us to come use the pool for the day. Mike stayed behind to get some work done while the rest of us loaded ourselves into the truck and set out for the hour drive, one that was peppered with the typical complaints of "I'm hungry," "I'm thirsty," "My elbow hurts," and "Are we there yet?"

When the girls mercifully dozed off, Papa said, "So, I learned this morning what the two H-words are that aren't a good mix."

"And what are they?" I asked.

"Hemorrhoids and jalapeños." He chuckled. I instantly wanted to point out that jalapeños does not, in fact, begin with the letter H, but I somehow managed to bite my tongue. My father-in-law is at the age where much discussion revolves around the workings or failed workings of one's bowels. I'm used to hearing about how regular or irregular they are and can sometimes even guess just by his outward mood. I adore jalapeños, and we often eat them stuffed for dinner, but whenever we do, I know I will have to endure the morning-after conversation. When we were halfway to Cabo, Papa muttered, "But I guess jalapeños isn't technically an H-word."

"No," I whispered, striving to appear free of judgment. "No, it's not."

When Mike and I visited Cabo in our youth, it wasn't the Cabo of today. Beers and shots were still a dollar, and you could walk down the street at night without being offered cocaine and prostitutes. We don't really go out in Cabo at night anymore. It's not that Cabo is beneath us or that we don't like a night on the town drinking and dancing, because who doesn't love being strung up by your feet like a giant, tequila-drinking marlin, but we can no longer afford Cabo. Hanging out in bars with sombrero-clad Jell-O shot pushers and floors shellacked in spilled Sex on the Beach has ironically become very expensive.

Visits to Cabo are now designed with our kids in mind. We go for day trips and ignore the expensive nightlife. We go for use of a condo pool so that our kids get the opportunity to swim. They're still too small to last long in the ocean and are far from being able to handle the ocean on their own. But at the condo pool, we can swim and relax and eat tacos poolside.

Not that a parent with small children in a pool can relax. It's not as if they frolic on their own or play a game of pool volleyball while I lounge with a book and a piña colada. This is one area that Sandi got right, teaching her girls to swim early. Both Bella and Rosie are "water safe," meaning they can be on their own and, short of a coconut falling on their head and knocking them unconscious, they're going to be just fine. Part of what I believe helped Bella and Rosie become water safe isn't just swimming lessons and the like, but Sandi's reaction to them when they're in the water. When my children are in the water and one of them looks in distress, or even just suffers an errant splash of water in the face, I stupidly rush to their aid, because I hate the water and am afraid of it myself. This has done nothing more than turn them into water wussies. I've made them just like me.

When Sandi and I were at a pool party together with all four girls, Rosie was swimming around and found herself in the deep end. She couldn't touch the bottom and started to panic. My instinct was to rush to her aid, but before I could do that, Sandi hollered instructions without moving to physically help her.

"Put your face in the water, Rosie," she said. This seemed to me the epitome of cruelty. If you're struggling in the water, do you really want your mother to tell you to put your face in it? Is this encouragement or designed to get the inevitable demise over with? Unlike me, Rosie fully understood and agreed with her mother. She put her face in the water and swam to a shallow area where she could again touch the bottom of the pool.

"I can't believe you just told your kid to put her face in the water," I said. "And that it worked."

"Well, you can't swim straight up and down. That's how people tire themselves out, trying to keep their head above water."

Because Sandi has me beat in this particular area of motherhood, her kids are now water safe, and she does spend her time by the pool lounging with a book and drinking a piña colada while I'm frantically tending to my water wussies with a dry towel when their eyes get wet.

I spent the day by the pool in Cabo doing just that, though I may have snuck in a bloody Mary or two while Nana took over a shift with the girls.

At the end of the day when we left Cabo to head back to Todos Santos, we had the obligatory Costco trip to make. Nana took the girls to the Costco snack stand while Papa and I did the shopping.

"Where should we go first?" I asked.

"Well…" Papa squinted down at his list. "Probably to the alcohol." We needed to stock up not just for ourselves, but also for the neighbors. It's common in Todos Santos to let your neighbors know when you'll be doing a Costco run and take orders. Chances are they'll repay the favor in one way or another. We made our way to the alcohol and loaded up the cart with five bottles of tequila, three Controy, two vodka, and three rum. And we're not talking fifths, either. You can't buy a small anything at Costco, including booze. We proceeded with the rest of our shopping, only to realize that our cart now made an ungodly racket of clanking bottles.

"This is almost embarrassing," I said to my father-in-law.

"Pretend you don't hear it," he advised.

"What?"

"Just pretend you don't hear it and that there's nothing to be embarrassed about. Believe me, I do it all the time."

We finished the shopping and made our way to the snack area to retrieve Nana and the girls.

"Oh dear," I said as we approached. When we'd left Todos Santos that morning, I'd dressed the girls in their swimsuits and sundresses. When we left the pool, I'd removed their wet suits and put their dresses back on, but I'd neglected to pack any underpants. Emilia was fine, her dress reaching her knees, but Ivy's was a bit shorter. On top of the lack of length, she was crawling up and down the picnic benches to amuse herself, in and among various shoppers stopping to enjoy a quick lunch. She wasn't oblivious to the fact that her bum-bum and hoo-hoo were on display; she was oblivious to the fact that there's anything wrong with having your bum-bum and hoo-hoo on display.

"Yeah," Nana said as we approached, "it's been a bit of an issue." Nana appeared resigned to the situation.

"Ivy!" I snapped. "Come here. Stop crawling around. Please just stand here for a second. It's almost time to go." She did as she was told and stood by my side. Nana and I chatted for a moment about plans for the evening. After a few minutes, Nana looked down, and her face took on a pained expression, somewhere between embarrassment and amusement. I looked down to see that Ivy had continued to obey and stood relatively still by my side. But she was also chewing on the hem of her dress, which meant that it was hiked up and held in place underneath her armpits. "Ivy!" I barked again.

"Put your dress down. That's bad manners." I turned to Nana. "Okay, I have to get these girls out of here. I'll take them to the car, and we'll meet you there whenever you guys are ready."

"Sounds good," said Nana with a slight smirk on her face. This is the smirk that grandparents are permitted in such situations, because while they are associated with the offending party, they take comfort in the fact that they are not ultimately responsible.

* * *

CHAPTER THIRTEEN

Mexican Montessori

I cannot fathom why a child wouldn't be ecstatic when presented with a quesadilla. It's a tortilla filled with melted cheese. I mean, come on, does life get any better? But while Emilia and Ivy would occasionally dig into this little carb- and fat-laden delight, at other times they'd refuse, demanding a diet with little reach beyond macaroni and cheese, hot dogs, and chicken nuggets.

"Mom, I don't like this quesadilla," Emilia complained. "It's different."

"Yeah, you know why it's different?" I asked. "Because it's *better*. That quesadilla is even better than the quesadillas we have back home." Which was true. You could fill a homemade tortilla like the kind we ate in Todos Santos with gravel, and it would still taste fantastic.

"I want noodles," Ivy said, referring to her budding addiction to all things Ramen.

"Come on, girls. We're in *Mexico!*"

They answered with hurt faces, looking at me as if I'd placed a pig's foot on a plate and expected them to gnaw on it.

I don't blame my children for being difficult when it comes to the kitchen. I take full responsibility for turning them into the picky little monsters that they are. And I look forward to when they grow beyond this stage, when we can go out together for sushi and I don't have to make sure that all of the dishes I serve at our dinner table are sufficiently bland. One day the Sriracha, my dearest hot sauce from Huy Fong Foods, Inc., will again flow freely, and I'll no longer have to buy ketchup in bulk.

In Mexico, the finicky nature of our children's palates was made more difficult by our lack of a kitchen. Our accommodations were rent free, but in order to get such a deal, you have to sacrifice things like frying pans and freezers. My in-laws put together a makeshift outdoor kitchen, which included a working sink, microwave, and toaster oven, but it still felt a bit like three months of camping. As a result, we sent the girls over to Nana and Papa's house every morning, where the grandparents prepared breakfast for them. Papa adopted the role of pancake maker and served the girls pancakes in the shapes of turtles, sharks, and caterpillars. This was an ideal arrangement until I realized that my children were consuming their own bodyweight in syrup on a daily basis.

"I'm really grateful that you're getting up at 6:30 every morning to essentially parent our kids," I said to Nana. "But I wonder if it's possible tomorrow to have something other than pancakes."

"Of course," she said. "What else do they like?"

"They're a lot less finicky when it comes to breakfast," I said. "So they'll eat pretty much anything."

"Anything?"

"Anything."

"Okay, like scrambled eggs?"

"Except for scrambled eggs."

"Oh."

"But they'll eat cereal, oatmeal, toast, yogurt, bagels, any of that stuff."

"Okay," she agreed. "We'll take a break from pancakes."

The next morning, I delivered the girls to Nana and Papa, went to ready myself for the day, and then retrieved them to get them dressed for school.

"Mom, guess what we had for breakfast!" Emilia was breathless with excitement.

"I don't know," I admitted.

"You have to guess, Mom," Ivy demanded.

I played along and named all of the things that Nana and I had talked about. They shook their heads no. The girls were so excited about whatever they'd had that I wondered if Nana hadn't mistakenly served them crack for breakfast.

"I'm tired of guessing," I said. "Just tell me."

They looked at each other with mischievous smiles and then, with a flourish of arm waving a la Vanna White, announced in unison: "Chocolate chip waffles with syrup!"

I looked to Nana, who stood off to the side, her posture suggesting she anticipated a whack on the nose with a rolled up newspaper.

"Tomorrow they'll have yogurt, bananas, and toast," she said. "I promise."

We weaned the children from syrup and for a while had them on a routine of toast with a glass of milk. Nutella and

Nesquik somehow made their way into the kitchen, and soon the girls were demanding chocolate toast with chocolate milk on a regular basis.

"No more chocolate toast," I declared one morning in frustration.

"Want me to make them pancakes?" Papa offered.

"Yes, please," I conceded.

* * *

As soon as breakfast was over, Ivy would immediately begin inquiring about the contents of her lunch. She was entering the stage of constant complaints of hunger, which I much prefer when compared to her previous stage, which was a full year of complaining of stomach pain.

"She's constantly telling me that her tummy hurts," I'd told the pediatrician while we were still in the U.S. "She says it maybe thirty times a day."

A lengthy discussion of Ivy's eating, drinking, and pooping habits followed, all of which were normal.

"I also just want to make sure there's nothing wrong with her appendix," I added.

"What makes you suspect the appendix?" the pediatrician asked.

"My husband's appendix burst when he was eighteen months." Mike still has a sizable scar from the resulting operation, which is a great prop for stories he tells the children about fighting off bears during his childhood in Alaska.

"Appendicitis is not hereditary," the pediatrician said.

"I know, but that would just be a really shitty coincidence."

She kneaded Ivy's abdomen for a while before delivering her diagnosis.

"There's nothing physically wrong with her," she said. "But keep in mind, toddlers don't always know how to express themselves. And they relate almost everything through their stomachs. When she says her tummy hurts, she might just be trying to communicate something she's feeling. 'My tummy hurts' could also mean 'I'm tired' or 'I'm hot.' Since she doesn't have a fully formed vocabulary for all of these things, that could be her fallback phrase." I was shocked by the wisdom of what she said and developed a new appreciation for doctors who take a moment to think beyond the physical symptoms.

Even after Ivy developed a full vocabulary to communicate what she was feeling at any given time, she did not give up the habit of having a fallback phrase just so that she constantly had something to say. By the time we'd arrived in Mexico, she'd given up on "My tummy hurts" and replaced it with "I'm hungry." The commute to school every morning was accompanied by Ivy's assessment of the contents of her lunch, an agenda of the order in which she'd consume the contents, and a firm reprimand to me for not including a *laster*.

"What is a *laster*?" I asked.

"A *laster* is the yummy sweet thing that you're supposed to eat last," Emilia explained.

"You mean like a dessert?"

"Yes, Mom," Ivy confirmed. "But it's not called dessert, it's called a *laster* because you eat it *last*. And you were supposed to put one in my *lunch*."

"You eat too much sugar as it is. I'm not sending you to school every day with a dessert."

The girls spoke in unison: "It's a *laster!*" Ivy threw her hands up in frustration, and Emilia rolled her eyes. Despite their exasperation, I was proud of their linguistic ingenuity, as *laster* seemed reminiscent of "traveler," also known as "booze in a travel coffee mug." I also felt relief that by *laster* they were referring to something more along the lines of Twinkies than port wine.

* * *

Every time my children attend a new facility in my absence, be it school, daycare, a playground, or someone's house for a play date, I experience the same nervousness as the first day of kindergarten. It never gets easier. The feeling was compounded when we sent them to a new place in a foreign country. But we'd toured the Montessori school on our last trip to Mexico and had been incredibly impressed with the school room as well as with the head teacher. What I liked about Mary in particular was that she talked to kids the way adults talk to one another. She didn't engage in baby talk or in any way try to dumb down her conversation when interacting with them. I was confident that she wouldn't offer my kids *wawa* or ask them if their lunch was really *nummers*. Her nature was somewhat serious, but I suspected that parents were more intimidated by this than students.

The commute to school involved two left turns down a dirt road and parking by the big cactus. Parents were not allowed to enter through the gate into the school grounds. Mary took charge of them at the gate, and the parents left. I don't think this was in order to hide from the parents that the children were thrown into a dungeon or put to work shoveling coal, but instead to curb the amount of tears in the morning, much like Ms. Sherod's approach on the first day of kindergarten. The number of tantrums and tearful goodbyes was kept to a minimum because the drop off was short and sweet and like clockwork.

On the first day of school, I had to fill out paperwork, which was charming. Instead of questions that I can't answer and therefore make me feel like a horrible mother, such as "What is your child's blood type and social security number?", this school required only the children's full names, birth dates, and a phone number so they had someone to call in case of emergency. I wasn't even required to list an address, which is good considering that my in-laws didn't have an address. I would have had to write something like: the casita with the green door down the street from the market where the dog always hangs out on the roof.

When I finished filling out the paperwork, I looked up and tried to locate my children. I expected hugs and kisses and perhaps Ivy clinging to my leg in an affectionate but leech-like manner because she couldn't bear the thought of me leaving her in this strange new place. But that was not the case. Instead, while I'd listed all the pertinent information, they'd made friends and run off to explore.

"Well, I guess they'll be just fine," I said, still looking around and trying unsuccessfully to locate them. Then I raised my voice in the hopes they might hear me. "I'll just go then, and Emilia and Ivy will have a great day." I scoured the grounds, expecting to see them emerge and run to me, pleading for a final hug and kiss, but I met only the assured gaze of Mary.

"They'll be just fine." She smiled.

And they were fine, and the school was wonderful, despite the fact that the school cat bit Emilia. It wasn't a bad bite, nothing that required medical attention, and Emilia learned, albeit the hard way, that most animals do not enjoy having a five-year-old wrap a pink ribbon around their ears, no matter how darling the end result may be. The school grounds included a playground, but not the metal and plastic monstrosities that are often found in the U.S., or even in the public playgrounds in Mexico. The playground was minimalist and endearing and somehow reminded me of the simplicity of children at play. It's good to remember that children are quite capable of playing with a stick and a rock, and don't require video games or even remote-control cars. Mexico often reminded me of this when we'd drive into town but have to wait at some point because two boys were playing soccer in the street with a "ball" made from an old milk carton, crushed into a shape as close to spherical as possible.

On one side of the Mexican Montessori sat a small garden where the children ostensibly assisted in cultivating plants and learning the biology behind the process. Nearby was a yellow brick road, and along this path the children constructed life-sized characters from *The Wizard of Oz*. The only negative about the school was the treacherous flight of stairs leading up to the main school room. But parents weren't around when the children went up and down the stairs, so they were more likely to behave under the guidance of Mary, who firmly reminded them of the importance of being careful and using the handrail.

When we first toured the school the year prior, deciding if this would indeed be "good enough" for our children, which is pompous at best, I was nervous about entering that main school room. What would it be like? A long metal table with chairs chained to the floor? A bare room with sparse walls and a glaring lack of functioning school supplies? And when had I become such a condescending asshole? The school room was a wondrous place, neat and tidy, but still brimming with supplies and projects and lessons of all kinds. A giant mural covered one wall, and Mary explained that the children had decided to do a project on whales. One section of wall detailed different types of whales, and another described their diet and life cycles.

"Jesus," I muttered to Mike. "I feel like I should go brush up on my whale knowledge."

"No kidding," he said. "This is amazing."

It's difficult dropping your child off when you see another child throwing a monumental tantrum. This happened at the Montessori school about a month into our stay, regardless of Mary's attempts at streamlining the drop-off process. One of the older girls, perhaps around seven or eight, was kicking and screaming and red in the face. Crying out that she just wanted one more hug. Mary literally wrestled the girl to the ground. The mother turned her back and walked away. This might seem cold and heartless, until you realize that the mother had probably been giving "one more hug" for the previous twenty minutes. Far better to rip the bandage off at once and get the pain over with than drag it out into something excruciating. While Mary physically restrained the screaming child, I said very quietly to Emilia and Ivy, "This girl is having a hard time today, so I just want you two to go ahead and go straight upstairs." Often they want to talk to Mary at the gate and tell her what they had for breakfast or what they dreamt about or what they get to do after school, but Mary had her hands full. The girls did what they were told, and by the time the mother of the distressed child had returned to her car, Mary had miraculously calmed the girl and was walking her inside.

Nothing about the Mexican Montessori was anything less than a school in the U.S. Nothing about it was settling for the Mexican equivalent or lowering our standards for whatever was the best we could find in Mexico. And again I was reminded of that American ego that assumes there is only one way and one place in which to live.

I can't deny that we did lower our standards somewhat when it came to things like car seats. Over the years, I've mellowed out in terms of transportation of my children, recognizing with each trip south that driving down a dirt road in Todos Santos is far safer than taking my children to school in Boise, where they are buckled and harnessed, but the trip to school requires navigating the roads with many other drivers, all traveling fast. Todos Santos is, for the most part, a sleepy little town, and the commute was a quiet and brief one. Because of that, I occasionally transported my kids to and from their Mexican Montessori school in the dune buggy. This was one of those combinations of words that my children simply could not master. Much like "hot tub," which Ivy referred to as "tub tub," Emilia was incapable of repeating "dune buggy," though it was by far her favorite vehicle. She called it the *dune truck, dump truck,* or *dung buggy,* anything other than dune buggy. The dune buggy was fun. It was open and bumpy, and while it may have been less safe than Nana and Papa's giant truck, it was fine for the short trip down a dirt road to the school.

Our time in Mexico required a lot of shuffling of vehicles to accommodate us, a family of four that arrived by plane with enough money for three months of food, but not for three months of a rental car. I'm always amazed at how willing people are to help us out. Not just Nana and Papa who handed over their car keys whenever we needed them, but also the neighbors, Tim and Melissa, people we'd just met. They had an extra, under-used vehicle, which the girls named "Monster Truck," and they were kind enough to essentially give it to us for the duration of our three-month stay.

Some mornings included complex discussions of who needed what car and when.

"I'm taking the girls to school in the Monster Truck," I said to Papa, "and Nana took your truck into town."

"So I'm without wheels for the time being?" he asked.

"Well, no," I said. "You have the dune buggy if you want to go to town."

His face immediately darkened.

"I am not driving that fucking dune buggy," he said.

My father-in-law is not what I would describe as a potty mouth. I'm far more crass than he is, so when he used the f-word in relation to the dune buggy, I detected real animosity. This stemmed from the fact that he was constantly driving somewhere to rescue Nana, who adored the dune buggy and used it to get to yoga class or one of the five million Zumba classes she taught every week. She loved the dune buggy. She looked cool in the dune buggy, and she knew it. But the dune buggy was less than reliable. On occasion, the ignition fell out, though it screwed back in with little problem. We also kept a large rock on the floor of the dune buggy so that when it wouldn't start, the rock was there to pound on the battery connection, which worked like a charm every time. But the dune buggy was, at heart, a Volkswagen, and anyone who has ever owned a Volkswagen knows that it's a love-hate relationship, because there comes a point when a roll of duct tape to keep the engine together no longer does the trick.

We took the dune buggy one afternoon to a restaurant down the street that had a band playing. It was an outdoor, kid-friendly place, half restaurant and half jungle-like garden. When we first arrived, I immediately purchased something for the children. I do this often, hoping that if they have something to eat or drink, then everything will be okay. I settled on orange juice. It was freshly squeezed, perhaps the most delicious orange juice on the planet, but the children didn't like it because it apparently wasn't processed, and they only like their food with heavy doses of additives and preservatives. They saw someone else eating a chocolate chip cookie, and I caved and ordered them each a cookie. Two cookies as big as their heads arrived, and they were happy. I'm sure other patrons looked over to see the children with their giant cookies and enormous glasses of orange juice and wondered at the intelligence of my decision, but when we're out at restaurants, I often panic and just start buying things. The cookies did the trick, and the girls relaxed.

Nana and Papa showed up, and we ordered a round of beer. The band was just warming up, doing a few sound checks. The female singer would sing into the mic: "This is a check, one two three, still checking, one two three." Even though it was only a sound check, she sang the words, and Nana, who is incapable of not dancing and clapping along when there's anything remotely similar to music in the air, began swaying her hips and clapping loudly. She has the loudest clap on the planet, which my husband inherited. When there's music playing, and my husband claps along, I'm often tempted to ask him if he can clap a little quieter, because it actually hurts my ears. The band did its sound check, abruptly stopped, and there was Nana in the middle of the restaurant swaying and clapping.

"Nana," I said, "it was just a sound check."

"Oh." She smiled. "You know me. I just can't help myself."

The guitarist strummed a few notes, and Nana leapt into a little shimmy accompanied by her famous and piercing clap. The notes trickled up into the air as the sound check stopped, leaving the restaurant once again to the slight din of people chatting and glasses clinking, save for the continued clap of Nana.

"Still just a sound check," I said.

"Well, now they're just teasing me."

Even in an elevator, with actual *elevator music* playing, Nana will dance and clap along. I'm a witness.

The band eventually played their music, and the children finished their cookies and went to play with other kids who were running around the garden. For a brief, delusional moment, I indulged in the fantasy that the children would play happily, and we adults could sit and listen to music and relax. But then I reminded myself that such flights of fancy do not live in the same world that I inhabit. I went to check on the kids, and sure enough, Emilia was tagging along with the group while Ivy stood in a miserable puddle of tears, either frightened or with hurt ego that the other children seemed capable of having so much fun without her. I calmed her down, and she insisted on returning to the group of children. I went back to the table and sat for a few minutes before again checking. It was the same situation. I calmed her down and asked if she wanted to sit with me or to dance with Nana. She pleaded with me to return to the other kids. It crossed my mind that another parent might sit at the table and enjoy the ignorance of their distressed child by listening to the band and just hoping things would work themselves out. Some parents might even argue that this would be better parenting, but that's not me. When the situation repeated itself a third time, I announced to the group at large that it was time for me to take the children home.

"I'll just take the dune buggy, and you guys can stay as long as you like," I said. They had arrived in the truck.

"Well, Amanda," said Nana, "the dune buggy doesn't have lights."

"Okay, well, all the more reason for me to go right now then." The sky was taking on a darker shade of blue.

"Show her that the lights don't work," Papa told Nana.

"Yes," said Nana, "I'll walk you out and show you that the lights don't work."

"I believe you," I told Nana.

"Amanda," Mike chimed in. "The dune buggy doesn't have any lights."

The sky was growing dimmer by the second, but the drive home was only three minutes.

"I know, Mike, and that's why I'm leaving now. Girls, come on. Let's go for a dune buggy ride." I grabbed them by the hands, and we walked to the gravel parking lot behind the restaurant.

Nana trailed with a look of concern. "Let me show you right here," she said when we reached the dune buggy. "Here are the lights that don't work."

"Yes," I said, "I can see that."

"See how they don't work?"

"Yes, I see that they don't work."

"So I'm not sure that you should go because it's going to be getting dark soon."

"That's why I'm going right *now*," I said.

"Okay, well just make sure you drive slow." I knew this was out of pure concern for the welfare of her daughter-in-law and granddaughters, but I saw the only result of driving extra slow being that we would end up driving in the dark. Without lights.

I had just enough light, and we made it back fine, though I decided that I would no longer drive the dune buggy if night was approaching, to avoid both the danger and the ridiculous conversation about it.

* * *

CHAPTER FOURTEEN

Smile for the Camera

The kids had a two-week break over Christmas. About the same time, Mike found an online discount for an all-inclusive resort in San Jose del Cabo. I had always wanted to go to an all-inclusive resort, to pay upfront for the stay and not worry about the bar bill at the end of the night or stress over the fact that I really wanted to order the lobster. It would solve the problem of the guilt I feel when Mike and I go out to dinner, and I order the filet mignon, and he orders a side salad.

"Are you worried about money?" I'd ask.

"What are you talking about?"

"I just ordered the filet, and you ordered a side salad."

"I'm not that hungry," he'd say. "I just really feel like a small salad."

"You eat mass quantities of food, and you're Alaskan. You gnaw on venison jerky and complain that my meatloaf isn't meaty enough. There's no way you just want a side salad."

"Really, I'm fine. Just get whatever you want." This was a pointless statement, as this conversation would occur after the orders were placed, and I'd feel a very public shame when the waiter would deliver our plates, placing a hunk of meat and baked potato in front of me and lettuce topped with a shredded carrot in front of my husband.

We packed for three nights at the resort, which would help break up the kids' two weeks of vacation. While I love Todos Santos, it is incredibly quiet, and there are only so many activities you can do with children, at least with children who don't last very long at the beach. Not only would the resort have heated pools, but also a kids' club.

Nana dropped us off at the resort in San Jose del Cabo, and we checked in. While it wasn't all-out luxury, it was very nice. We had a room with two double beds, which meant there wouldn't be much in the way of evening intimacy, but that's what couples with young children agree to deal with on three-day resort vacations. I've always thought of life as cruel in that regard, that you have to have sex to make children, who then routinely rob you of the opportunity to have sex. Still, the room had a lovely view of the resort's pools leading out to the beach.

I am not a pool person. I don't enjoy swimming, and I don't enjoy being wet or cold. But a heated pool makes all the difference. Conversely, Mike, who in the past has been the tough one when it comes to entering the water, turned wimpy on me.

"What's wrong?" I said. "It's warm." I was already in the water with both girls, but he was still struggling to make it down the pool stairs.

"It's not as warm as I want it to be," he said. And I realized then that Mike might be tough when the water is genuinely cold, but if it's heated, he wants it to feel like a giant hot tub.

"Oh, just get in," I said.

He took a step down, and the water was up to his calves, then his knees, then his thighs. Then he gritted his teeth and cringed, whimpering ever so slightly as he took another step and the water passed crotch level.

We spent hours swimming with the girls but then got a break while they went to play at the kids' club. We drank by the pool with limited guilt because we'd actually been engaged and conscientious parents for a few hours before shipping them off.

"We might need to make reservations for dinner," Mike mentioned as we lounged in the sun.

"Why?" I asked. "Can't we just go wherever?"

"Well, I heard someone mention that the restaurants fill up, so if you don't have a reservation, you get stuck with the buffet."

"Oh dear god, you know how I feel about buffets."

"I'm sure it's a nice buffet," Mike said. "I'm sure it's not like a gross buffet."

"It's not a nice versus gross issue," I said. "It's the *principle.*"

"It's interesting to me that you're disturbed by the concept of all you can eat, but you don't seem to have any problem with all you can drink."

"I'm sorry, what were we talking about? I believe you were going to see about dinner reservations."

That evening, we arrived promptly at six at the Italian restaurant where Mike had reserved a table for four. A waiter led us to a table set with wine glasses and linens.

"Crap," I whispered to Mike.

"Don't worry," he assured me. "We'll just do the best we can."

"Okay, but if it all goes to shit, we're just going back to the room and ordering room service."

"Agreed."

Our nervousness was due to the fact that we'd never tried to dine with a three-year-old and a five-year-old in a restaurant that nice. Any time we'd taken them to a restaurant that was at least decent, they had paper placemats with crayons and cups made out of plastic. This place appeared to have no such things, and the waiters presented both Emilia and Ivy with ice water served in glass goblets. Mike gave the girls a stern warning about how this was a special place and we needed good behavior. I silently conceded that we should have just gone with the buffet. But both girls managed to drink their water without soaking the table or breaking a glass. We were tantrum free, and at no time was pasta thrown on the walls or floor.

The next night was Mexican fiesta night, which included a piñata for the children and a show with traditional Mexican dancers. I was scared about how the piñata would go, anticipating tears or toddlers coming to blows. But it was incredibly well organized. All of the children were lined up on stage from youngest to oldest to make sure everyone had a turn. A man in the background pulled the piñata up when it looked in danger of breaking and lowered it down for the little ones who had more difficulty, ensuring that everyone got a turn and everyone was happy. He timed it perfectly so that the piñata broke on the last child's turn.

"Here come the tears," I said to Mike as the children scrambled for candy. But again, the staff knew what they were doing. Everyone was well behaved, everyone got candy, and my kids survived without crying and without punching anyone else's child in the face, which counts as a win in my book. Then the dancers began, and once again my expectations were exceeded. They put on a wonderful show with talent and skill. When the show was over, they invited people from the crowd to meet the dancers and have their pictures taken with them.

"Emilia," I said, "go up there and say *gracias.*" Emilia, more often than not, does things like this when I ask her to, and she went up on the stage and said *gracias* to one of the male dancers. I followed, and the dancer crouched down and sat Emilia on his knee, then turned to me and smiled, ready for their picture to be taken. The only problem was that I didn't have our camera on me at the time. Emilia and the dancer smiled, held still, and waited.

"Just give him a hug, Emilia." They continued waiting, frozen in place. "I, uh, I don't have a camera," I said. But it seemed that the two of them had an unspoken agreement to wait and remain perfectly still until I took their picture. A minute passed with them looking at me, the perfect picturesque pair. "Okay," I said. "Good job, everybody. Emilia, you can come down now." No response as they continued to wait. "Okay, then," I said, and I literally held up my hands and pantomimed holding a camera. "One, two, three." I pressed an imaginary button and said, "Click." And I felt like a complete moron, but apparently this did the trick because the spell was broken, and they shook hands and parted company as if I had actually taken a picture. I can only imagine what the Mexican dancer thought of me, perhaps that I struggled with a traumatic brain injury or something of the like. Hopefully he chalked it up to advances in technology that have produced such wonders as an invisible camera.

The next day, we sat by the pool, and I recognized a family that had been seated next to us that first night at the Italian restaurant. We'd shared a look that night of mutual under-standing and fear. They had three young children and were equally nervous about how to make it through a meal at a restaurant that didn't have plastic cups with straws for the kids. They, too, had survived. That night, they'd mentioned that they were going to "get a discount" on a fishing expe-rience. I was familiar with what "get a discount" meant. It meant sitting through a three-hour timeshare pitch. I'm always shocked by the people who are willing to endure this. I know that three hours is an entirely survivable length of time, but not when an accomplished salesperson spends all 180 minutes approaching you as a deal that needs to be closed. I hate saying no when someone wants me to say yes. It's raw conflict veiled in niceties, and I'd almost rather just arm wres-tle for it. The winner gets my credit card. But others don't view sales pitches with the same sense of dread that I do, and if you sat through the pitch, you got a deal on one of the activities available. Because while the term "all-inclusive" may refer to all your meals and drinks, it does not go so far as to include excursions like reeling in a marlin or swimming with Flipper.

The couple smiled when they saw me, and I walked over to say hello. "Hey, how are you guys?" I asked.

"Great," the wife replied.

"You didn't buy a timeshare, did you?" I laughed.

Their faces dropped a little. "Actually, we did," she conceded.

"Oh, uh, I mean, uh, congratulations!" I patted the husband on the arm. "I'm sure that's a great decision, and it will work out wonderfully for you." It was a pathetic and obvious back pedal, but they laughed.

"We've sat through a handful of these pitches before and never considered it," she confided in me. "But for some reason, this time it felt like the right thing to do."

"We're going to grab some lunch," the husband said. "Do you guys want to join us?"

"No thanks," I answered. "We just ate, and I still have my foot in my mouth, in any case."

* * *

Upon our return to Todos Santos, we once again had to constantly employ bug spray. Immediately after a shower, I'd coat myself in it. It was like scrubbing myself clean and then bathing in grease. And how is it that one mosquito could bite me a dozen times? I mean, how much blood can they actually store in their tiny little insect bodies? And do they gravitate to me, in particular, because my blood contains a higher concentration of alcohol?

One of the great benefits of living in Mexico was that it was somehow acceptable to drink every day. Sure, I drank every day at home, too, but it was much more regulated. In Boise, I only drank after five p.m. because that's when I had picked up my kids from daycare, arrived home with them, and knew I wouldn't have to drive anywhere else. Fine, I've had the occasional midday glass of wine or beer, but generally alcohol consumption was limited to the evenings. Part of what changed this in Mexico was that I rarely had to drive, and if I did, I had the kids safely home from school before two p.m. This left a full afternoon with which to nurse a few beers before the real evening indulgences of margaritas began.

A margarita in Mexico is far superior to what passes for the same thing in the States. If someone is using margarita mix, you should run away very fast. The people who market and sell margarita mix should face punishment from the Food and Drug Administration, or maybe from the Bureau of Alcohol, Tobacco, and Firearms. The charges should be for them defiling and disgracing a wonderful drink and passing their product off with false advertising. A true margarita should contain a little bit of orange liqueur, but that's not the chief ingredient, and nothing about it should be sickly sweet or syrupy. I adore margaritas so much that it's difficult for me not to order them in a nice restaurant, but getting served a fake margarita is devastating at the first sip. I'm not saying there's only one way to make a margarita. In fact, I regularly enjoy slight variations on the drink. I'll go for a Cadillac or a jalapeño margarita any day. But the basic ingredients that you start with should be tequila, orange liqueur, and fresh lime juice. Anyone who offers to make a margarita but doesn't have a lime squeezer is highly suspect. I also enjoy adding the occasional splash of orange juice or a little club soda.

Drinking a margarita in Mexico, which implies a genuine margarita, should not be taken lightly. I'm incapable of having just one, but I will be unquestionably buzzed after two. The best course of action for me is to have two but then switch to beer for the rest of the evening. I can manage this and still be functioning the following day without wanting to take my own life. If I have three or more margaritas, I am destined to make a grand fool of myself at some point in the course of the evening. Some people would say that having three margaritas is the same as having three drinks, and if I'm trashed after three drinks, I must be a lightweight. But I think a good margarita is made with roughly twice the alcohol that I put in any other mixed drink. And the other mixed drinks I make are usually doubles. So far from being a lightweight, I'm actually an incorrigible lush.

Two of our favorite people on the planet to drink margaritas with are Chris and Elizabeth. Ten years prior, we met Chris and Elizabeth during a brief trip to Todos Santos. We had no children at the time and no intention of having children. Something about Chris and Elizabeth began to alter our thinking. Before meeting them, I'd always thought that once you have kids, you have to stop engaging in any adult fun and instead learn to sew. After all, isn't that what moms do? Sew buttons on things and make Halloween costumes? But Elizabeth, mother to a two-year-old and a five-year-old at the time, never seemed to be sewing, often had a drink in hand, yet still seemed to be a fantastic parent. How could this be? We met them at a party at their home in Mexico, and it was fully an adult party. Not like you had to surrender your keys at the door or hold a camera while someone made a snuff film or anything like that, just the type of party where adults drink alcohol, and no one presents a cake in the shape of a Disney character.

Yet their children were present, having fun and playing, but without requiring constant attention from their parents. The home was filled with lit candles, and a large cactus punctuated their back patio, which ended with a treacherous looking set of concrete stairs. At first I was terribly worried and thought I should somehow intervene, step in and save these children who appeared in immediate danger. Surely a child would inexplicably fling his body into the giant cactus and get stuck there. And undoubtedly someone would need stitches by the end of the evening after plummeting down the concrete stairs of death. What horrors awaited when a toddler attempted to play in the hot wax pool of a giant candle?

"Oh my gosh," I said to Elizabeth. "How do you keep your kids safe with all these candles around?"

"What do you mean?" She looked at me with a puzzled expression.

"Aren't you afraid someone's going to get burned?"

"Um, no," she answered. "We just tell the kids not to touch the candles."

"What about the cactus?" I asked. "And the stairs? How do you keep them from falling into the cactus or falling down the stairs?" As we spoke, the children chased each other in circles around the cactus and then ran another loop that came frighteningly close to the stairs.

"Well, uh, we tell them to be careful. And really, when you're in Todos Santos, it's the adults you have to worry about, not the children."

She was right, I realized, as I looked around to see adults holding beer bottles, margaritas, and shot glasses. While the children might be children, they were entirely sober, in superior physical shape, and with better coordination than any of the adults at the party.

This shocked me. You could simply tell children not to do something, and they would listen? It seemed that most of the parents I'd been around created a padded-room-like environment to keep their kids from danger. The children I'd been around were always determined to put themselves at risk. Or at least behave in an unbelievably obnoxious way that made me never want to breed. But these kids were well behaved, listened to their parents, and were actually fun. And their parents seemed like fabulous people who managed to have a party and not bark at their children every two minutes. They put the idea of parenthood into a new light.

After that initial meeting, we deepened our friendship with Chris and Elizabeth when they moved to Boise for a few years. They became the friends that inevitably left us closing our eyes and shaking our heads because we found it hard to stand by and watch them make certain decisions. They were the wrong decisions, except for the fact that they always turned out to be right. For instance, after a few years in Boise, they decided to relocate to a new town. That's not such a big deal of course, but they had little money and no idea where that new town might be. They packed up a U-Haul and decided to start driving because, in the words of Elizabeth, "It just feels right." There's a somewhat romantic notion about pulling up roots and heading out to find a new home and a new start, but they did this with two small children in tow, the idea of which creates anxiety in me akin to the trepidation I'd feel at the prospect of an eyeball transplant or having to take a job at Chuck E. Cheese.

I am an extreme planner. Without the benefit of a plan, I feel lost and adrift and without purpose, which makes me uncomfortable. But every time Chris and Elizabeth take this sort of action, things work out just fine. Even *well*. Which means that they constantly rob me of the opportunity to say, "I told you so."

I'm not sure why I don't trust my own intuition as much as Chris and Elizabeth do theirs. It's amazing to me how self-assured they are. Especially in light of Elizabeth's background, you'd think she'd be more screwed up than most. She and seven siblings were sent to an Opus Dei school while growing up, which led to a lot of confusion later in life, like thinking that saying the word "sex" on the telephone was the same as having phone sex. When she first told me that she had been raised Opus Dei, I had no idea what she was talking about.

"You know," she said. "Like in *The Da Vinci Code.*"

"Holy crap, you mean like the whole self-flagellation thing? That beat-yourself-and-not-in-a-good-way religion?"

"Yep, that's the one."

"So, by all accounts, you should be completely messed up."

"Actually, I really liked school," she said. "Honestly, I have no complaints about it."

"Must be the brainwashing," I suggested.

"It's possible."

Instead of pledging her life to the church or rebelling against the strict teachings, Elizabeth managed to adopt only positive influences from this experience and then move on, which is how she operates in all aspects of her life. Not only are Chris and Elizabeth *not* Opus Dei subscribers, but I'd go so far as to describe them as unholy in all the right ways.

Chris has a shock of bleached blond hair that shoots from his head in all directions, along with a not-so-secret fantasy to be Billy Idol, which he acts out when sufficiently sauced. Elizabeth is short with black hair and deep blue eyes. When we first met Chris and Elizabeth, they had hair of a closer hue, but as the years passed, he bleached his ever blonder while she dyed hers ever blacker. When I first met them, I thought they were the most strikingly good-looking couple I'd ever seen.

Chris is often written off by people because they incorrectly assume that he's a stupid surfer dude. There are a lot of surfer dudes in Mexico, but I haven't yet met any stupid ones. And Chris, who doesn't surf all that often, is far from stupid. Unlike most people, he's content with having a good time and doesn't feel the need to go out of his way to prove to people that he's smart. Every now and then, I'll have a conversation with Chris that lets me know there's so much more to him than what appears on the surface. I gained an entirely new respect for him when he let me read an early draft of a young adult novel he'd written. Much of the content of the novel, not surprisingly, dealt with children learning how to cope with other people who write them off because of what they appear to be on the surface.

Elizabeth isn't written off in this manner, at least not as often as Chris. People correctly assume that she's intelligent, though this comes across without her having to go out of her way to convince them. She is relaxed and at peace with herself and often offers insights that let you know she's incredibly smart. But Chris occasionally appears to be a dumb blond. Not only does the color of his hair lead people to assumptions about him, but the fact that it's spiky acts to confirm it. It's almost like people assume flat hair keeps a person's brains in place.

Chris traveled into San Jose del Cabo one day to pick up a relative who had come to visit. On the way, he was pulled over by the Mexican feds. They removed him from his vehicle, made him put his hands on the car, and proceeded to search his wallet, pockets, and vehicle. Surely a guy with blond spiky hair in a black jeep was using drugs or trafficking in drugs or engaged in some other type of illegal activity that they could bust him for.

"What did you do?" I asked when he related this story. "Did you give them money?"

"No," he said, indignant. "I didn't give them any money because I didn't do anything wrong. At one point, they found a Halls wrapper and were sure it was some sort of drug paraphernalia. Then they asked me what COLTLUV means, as if it's some sort of drug gang symbol." Chris has a personalized license plate that reads COLTLUV. Rather than this being a sign of his involvement in an international drug ring, it is instead an indication of his undying love and allegiance for the Indianapolis Colts.

"So what happened?"

"They kept me there for forty-five minutes and searched every inch of me."

"Like a body cavity search?"

"*No*, not like a body cavity search. Amanda, why would you even ask that?"

"I don't know," I admitted. "I guess I've never known someone who's had one."

"Do you really think that if someone undergoes a body cavity search, they're going to want to tell you all about it?"

"Good point, though now I think you really did have a body cavity search, and this is your way of telling me that you don't want to tell me," I said.

"So *anyway*," Chris continued, "they searched my pockets,

my wallet, and everything in the car. But eventually they had to let me go because I didn't do anything wrong. I wasn't even speeding. My registration is up to date, I'm 100 percent kosher, but I think they were just shocked they didn't find drugs of some sort." At that moment, I was happy to know Chris and felt that he'd achieved a triumph for surfer dudes everywhere.

* * *

CHAPTER FIFTEEN

The Good Days

"Are you going to the pool party?" Elizabeth asked. Friends in the neighborhood were organizing a shindig.

"I don't know," I muttered. "I might have to... do some laundry or something."

"Their pool is heated," Elizabeth assured me.

"Okay, then yes, we'll be there."

My fear of being forced into situations where I will be wet and cold and have to pretend like it's fun is downright paralyzing. I don't understand why I'm so often alone in this. How is it that people are able to laugh and have fun while freezing to death? Is my layer of blubber somehow less effective at preserving body warmth than their layer of blubber?

We attended the pool party, and in addition to the pool being heated, Mike graciously took responsibility of the girls while they were in the water, thereby saving me the horror of having to get wet. Emilia and Ivy wore floaties, so a good time was had by all. Floaties these days are remarkably better designed than the pathetic little arm rings that were both popular and useless when I was a kid. Emilia and Ivy's floaties are actually approved by the U.S. Coast Guard as flotation devices. Nothing on this device is inflatable, and therefore nothing can pop. They allow our children a little bit of independence in the water, so they're a big hit.

At the pool party, the hosts had a few pool noodles lying around. This was Emilia's first experience up close and personal with a noodle, and she found it incredibly... enjoyable. Nana and I both noticed this.

"Boy, she sure likes that worm, doesn't she?" my mother-in-law said.

"Yes, she does. But you can't call it a worm, okay? It's a noodle. Nobody calls them worms."

"Oh right, a noodle. Well, she sure likes to ride that noodle."

It was true. While everyone else in the pool, including Chris and Elizabeth's older and therefore more appropriate children, had their noodles wrapped around their backs and coming underneath their armpits, so that they might lazily drift about, both Emilia and Ivy were straddling theirs and doing their best to bounce up and down in the water.

As we left, Emilia approached our host. "Where did you get that long pink thing?" she asked, indicating the noodle. "I *really* like that. Can you buy them at the store? How much do they cost?"

At home, Emilia continued on about the noodle. "I really liked that pink thing because it felt good on my pee-pee, and I could do that *all day*. It feels *so good*."

"Oh dear," said Mike. The first time your children utter these words, you're at a bit of a loss as to how to respond.

"I know it feels good, Emilia," I said. "And it's perfectly normal that things there feel good, but we don't need to tell everyone about it, okay?" Children so often don't understand this thinking. They are honest and brutal and can't fathom why it's okay to say that the sun feels good on your face but not that the noodle feels good on your hoo-hoo.

The next time we arrived at our friends' house for a pool party, they surprised the girls by having purchased each of them noodles of their very own.

Once children learn what feels good, everything becomes hump-worthy. At Chris and Elizabeth's house, one of their children had a giant stuffed banana. It's the sort of ridiculously exaggerated toy that one wins at a carnival, and Emilia loved that banana in more ways than one. She's perfectly normal in this regard, and I knew what to expect from watching my niece at that age and having to repeatedly ask her to cease humping the couch.

I know that overall I have it easy when it comes to kids in that I have only girls. I can only imagine the amount of penis fondling I'd have to witness if we had boys. On occasion, I've spotted a young boy in our Boise neighborhood who rides his bike to and from school. One day I saw him stopped at the side of the road with a confused look on his face. I pulled over and rolled down my window.

"Are you okay?" I asked. "Is something wrong with your bike?"

He turned to look at me and didn't answer. I noticed that while his feet were on the ground, straddling the bike, he used his hands on the handlebars to move the bike back and forth underneath him so that the seat of the bike massaged his crotch. He seemed incapable of speaking, and I suddenly felt like a pedophile.

"Oh, uh, okay then," I muttered dumbly. "Carry on." I rolled up my window and drove away.

* * *

When New Year's in Todos Santos rolled around, we readied ourselves to attend a notoriously delightful bash at the home of some friends. I used this particular party as an excuse to wear a little black dress that's a smidge too short and too tight, along with knee-high black leather boots. While this may sound as if I looked like a hooker, I contend that it was only slightly whorish, not completely whorish. My mother-in-law owns the exact same dress. It looks less whorish on her, in part because she's short and a more appropriate height for this particular dress. After Mike and I sufficiently primped for the evening, we entered Nana and Papa's house. I wore the little black dress, and Mike donned jeans and a white, buttoned-down shirt. We found Nana in the exact same dress, and Papa in jeans and a white, buttoned-down shirt. I wasn't sure if our matching was cute or pathetic.

"You look way better in this dress than I do," said Nana.

"That's not true," I countered. "You look like a million bucks. I look like a five-dollar hooker."

"Of course, we'd be twins like this." She looked from Mike to Papa. "We'd be two sets of twins."

"Dad," ordered Mike, "you need to change right now."

"Okay," Papa agreed.

"Yep," said Nana, staring unabashedly at my boobs, "I'm going to have to change, too." While my mother-in-law is in better shape than I'll ever be and looks fantastic, she's not overly abundant in the breast region. She didn't want to be caught standing next to me while wearing the identical dress, because in this particular dress, my boobs border on the obscene. It's not because they're actually all that big; it's that they appear enormous when you're doing everything you possibly can to suck in every inch of real estate your body has. You can't suck in your breasts or, unfortunately, any part of the neck and double chin area. But you can suck in your stomach, which I engage in with all the energy my chubby little physique can muster. When I do so, my breasts sometimes look a little bit porno in relation to the rest of my body. It's also the type of dress that prohibits any bending at the waist.

"If we dance at this party," I warned Mike, "and I'm not saying we will, you have to be conscious of how short this dress is."

"I promise."

"Because there is precious little real estate to work with here. You can twirl me, but I *must* remain upright at all times."

"Okay."

"And don't do that leg hump thing."

"What leg hump thing?"

"You know, where we dance, but you kind of have a leg in between mine so it looks a little bit like I'm humping your leg. That one. Don't do that."

"One, I have no idea what you're talking about." He knew exactly what I was talking about. "And B, even if I did know, why can't I do it?"

"Because it hikes my dress up, and I don't have an inch to spare. You show my panties to the crowd, and I will, literally, punch you in the crotch in front of your own parents."

"All right, all right, no leg hump thing."

"Thank you."

We did dance, just a few songs, but had a great time, and I think I survived without flashing my buttocks at anyone. Mike was very conscious of the length of the dress, and I only had to tell him twice that if he continued to spin me, I would surreptitiously knee him in the groin. He's a very good dancer and a very good lead. He knows how to swing and spin. The problem is that he often thinks it's funny to spin me repeatedly until I get to the point where I'm so dizzy I'm forced to threaten harming his genitalia.

The New Year's party has a tradition of drinking one shot of tequila every hour on the hour from seven p.m. to one a.m. This is optional, of course, but most of us do it, with only the occasional drink in between. We started this tradition years ago after the first party. That party started at seven o'clock as well, but we toasted with tequila shot after tequila shot— only to find that most of us were passed out by nine o'clock. The every-hour-on-the-hour method paces people, and we're more likely to make it to the New Year. After midnight, everyone is so proud of themselves for making it to midnight, the true overindulging begins. Thus, the majority of hangover creation occurs between midnight and one a.m.

There are always people who abstain from excessive drinking, which I applaud, as I seem incapable of doing so. And then there's the opposite end of the spectrum, those who ignore the shot-per-hour custom and dive headfirst into a bottle, where they're likely to have been marinating all day. These people may pass out early or fall into a fire pit or get caught puking in the kitchen sink. I never fault them for this, because I've been the drunken asshole at the party on many an occasion. Parenthood has helped temper my indulgence in vice somewhat, as I know that no matter how hung over I am, my children are still going to wake up at 6:30 the next morning.

The New Year's party was an odd mix of class and debauchery and a lot of fun. I felt successful because I remembered everything. I don't mind a hangover as long as my memories of the previous night are intact. When I have gaping holes in my recollection of an evening, I spend the next day mentally berating myself and wondering if it's time for rehab.

After Mike and I abandoned the dance floor, we could tell that the sobriety level of the crowd was quickly diminishing. People grew sloppier in their moves, and dancing couples morphed into a big circle of people dancing. I always find this awkward, because it essentially puts everyone on display since everyone is facing everyone else. But this is what happens when we all get drunk, and then those who are really drunk begin dancing in the middle of the circle, because having everyone facing you is no longer enough. You want a stage on which to display your moves, which look ridiculous except in your head where you are sexy and talented and coordinated. Chris became exceedingly drunk after midnight and spent much time dancing in the middle of the circle. And then he did the notorious Chris move; he took off his shirt. The channeling of Billy Idol began, and at one point he had a glow stick somehow attached to his nipple ring. The nipple ring is disconcerting. It's one of those things that I constantly forget that he has until we're at an epic bash and he gets drunk and takes off his shirt. When he's drunk enough for shirt removal, he's usually lost a good deal of his coordination. I'm always filled with fear that he's going to get his nipple ring caught on something.

"I should probably get him home," said Elizabeth in regards to Chris.

"Yes," I agreed. "That's probably a good idea. We'll see you at our place."

We would reconvene at our casita where Elizabeth's children had been babysitting Emilia and Ivy.

On the way home, Mike said to me, "You look fantastic."

"Thanks," I replied. "It's not easy holding in your stomach for six hours."

"And thanks for not punching me in the groin," he added.

"Happy New Year, sweetie."

* * *

CHAPTER SIXTEEN

Porky

Our trip to Mexico coincided with the second annual Todos Santos Por Que 5K, which I unfortunately always thought of as the Porky 5K, though this is attributable only to my own porkiness, not anyone else's. A 5K run is 3.1 miles. For someone who runs regularly, this is a nice, short, easy distance that you can do in less than half an hour. *I can do this*, I thought. *I run all the time.* Of course, this was after a month in Mexico, and I'd run only once so far during our trip, which hardly counts as running "all the time." But still, it's a manageable distance for someone who has been running for a few years, which I have, despite the continued presence of my potbelly. This belly has been sticking around for so long that it's almost time to name it.

It was a perfect morning for a 5K, a beautiful day but not too hot. Most races I've participated in have a warm up, and for some reason, this always seems to be an eighties themed warm up. In the case of the Por Que 5K, the warm up was led by a yoga instructor, which is a good representation of the town's laid back, feel good, slightly hippie-esque vibe. I wondered at how effective this slow and calm stretching would really be in terms of getting everyone warmed up for a race. But then the yoga instructor turned the microphone over to my mother-in-law, who proceeded to lead the crowd in an abbreviated session of Zumba.

Emilia stood next to me during the warm up and periodically announced to those around her with pride, "That's my Nana," and pointed to the stage. Nana has an energy that's contagious, and she's perfectly suited to this sort of thing. The crowd collectively danced and bounced with Nana, though there was one particular move that no one was capable of, and whenever she did it, the rest of us stopped and stared at her with a dumb look on our faces, waiting for her to return to a simpler maneuver we might be capable of.

When Zumba finished, it was time for the kids to run the 1K. My children were not a part of this particular event because they're still at the age when they walk for approximately thirty seconds before complaining that they're tired or their feet hurt and can someone please give them a piggy back ride? Instead, we watched the other participants, mostly kids between the ages of seven and twelve. Emilia is a perfect spectator. She is encouraging and a wonderful cheerleader, though I confess I have a bit of trepidation when admitting to myself that she might actually want to be a cheerleader in her teens. In my youth, I was frightened of cheerleaders. They seemed so foreign. They were pretty and popular and had bubbly personalities. Why didn't they have the same awkwardness I felt? Or share my fascination with serial killers and other evidence of man's inhumanity to man?

The kids took off and ran the 1K, which was apparently a bit of a debacle. The course wasn't clearly marked, and a few of the kids ended up unknowingly taking a shortcut. This, in turn, skewed the winners' list, though I assert that a child running a race should attempt to focus on finishing, not winning. Toward the end of the race, we saw a girl approaching the finish line with tears streaming down her face. She was walking and accompanied by an older girl who attempted to comfort her.

"Aw," Mike said in sympathy. "She must have fallen."

The girl didn't look scraped up or in any way hurt, and I offered my own theory. "Sometimes people have visions of winning these things, and then when the race starts and they take off, they find that it's more difficult than they thought. When other kids pass you, and you realize your daydreams aren't going to come true, it can be devastating." We watched the girl and, from her crestfallen look, figured this was probably the case.

With the 1K complete, it was time for the other runners to line up for the 5K. I said farewell to Mike, Emilia, and an exceptionally cranky Ivy and made my way to the starting line. The race began, and we took off. About a minute into the race, I spotted Nana and Papa, who were standing off to the side cheering everyone on. I made my way to the side of the course where they were so that I might get a high five from them as I passed. But as I approached them, I could tell that they somehow didn't see me.

"Hey!" I waved as I got closer. Still they didn't see me. As I passed by within inches of both of them, I pointed to Nana and said, "Hot stuff right here." Calling Nana "hot stuff" is usually a sure thing in terms of getting her attention, but still they neither saw nor heard me, despite the fact that I pretty much screamed in their faces. I smiled to myself at their seeming trance and continued on.

The first half of any race is usually one of anxiety and self-doubt, with phrases swirling in my head along the lines of "Why am I doing this?" and "I can't do this" and "Just give up now and go find a bloody Mary." I've run a handful of half-marathons and logically know that I'm completely capable of running a 5K, but no matter the length of the race, I will always spend the first half thinking these things. The second half of the race is the enjoyable part for me, if there's even going to be one. Once I hit the halfway mark, no matter the total distance, the doubt recedes, and I start to think opposite thoughts. "Of course I can do this" and "I'm awesome" and "When this is over, I'm going to go find a bloody Mary."

About a quarter of the way into the race, I spotted two of my fellow racers stopped along the side of the road. The woman was comforting the man, who was bent over and puking what appeared to be five gallons of coffee. I've heard of runners having a cup of coffee before a race, something to give them a little bit of a caffeine kick. And I've heard of runners over-hydrating with too much water, but I failed to see the wisdom in drinking excessive amounts of coffee before a race. I think the racer at that point also realized his error. Another drawback for me, at least, would be that drinking coffee inevitably makes me have to go to the bathroom, in more ways than one. I wondered at how much comfort he was receiving from the woman who was standing there rubbing his back. I know this is one of those instinctual things that people do to others who are throwing up, but I don't understand it. When I throw up, I absolutely do not want to be touched in any way. And having someone rub my back while I do it really just makes me want to throw up more.

I continued on and finished the race, though I did have to walk at one point up a very steep hill. It was a race where you had to always look at the ground in front of you. Even when the course traveled along the paved roads in town, these were still Mexican roads, and the potholes and opportunities to break an ankle were endless. I finished the race and saw that Chris had already made it back. Like me, Chris had taken up running when he quit smoking. In a way, running is literally a means of running away from addiction. Ex-smokers also run because we never could before, and we feel that we suddenly have to make up for the years where it was physically impossible to run for more than a few minutes. Not just because our lungs burned and pleaded with us to collapse, but also because after a few minutes, it would be time to stop and have another cigarette.

"Did you run too fast?" I asked Chris.

"Yes. You?"

"Yes," I admitted. There's a certain frenzy that comes from racing within a large group of people. It's equal parts pack mentality and ego. It's what drives us runners to move faster than we normally would and place ourselves in danger of burning out too soon and being unable to finish the whole race. And it's what drives non-runners to suddenly try it and end up puking along the side of the road.

"I kept telling myself to slow down, that I was going too fast. It's like I know I'm running too fast, but I can't help it," I said.

"I'm the same way," said Chris. "Plus, I think I had visions of winning."

This is another ridiculous thing for normal runners like Chris and me to think about. You can't help but fantasize that it might happen, just like the little girl who cried when she realized that others were faster. Chris and I run faster than many others out there, but we are by no means professional athletes or even above average. We have spare tires and too many late nights drinking. Even if a normal runner has an above average race, there will always be a freakishly fast handful of people who possess the ability to run three miles in a little over fifteen minutes. It's easy to forget about them during the race and indulge in the fantasy that you might come in first place— since during the race you can't even see them because they're so far ahead of you.

After the race, Mike took the girls home while Nana and I ran errands in town. Errands that did not include a bloody Mary but which may or may not have included two mimosas. One of our stops was the produce store in Todos Santos that's considered better than the little markets dotted throughout town that offer only weak and wilted greens. I'm a big fan of vegetables, not because I'm overly healthy, but because I miss them while we're in Mexico, often feeling like I'm drowning in a diet of alcohol, tortillas, and cheese. Don't get me wrong; I love alcohol, tortillas, and cheese, but inevitably I end up looking and feeling gross. I'd planned before this trip not to end up gross and instead committed myself to frequenting the good veggie place. Having just run a 5K and consuming a mere two mimosas seemed like a great time to continue an attempt at health and visit the produce store. I walked up the steps to Lizarraga and noticed some sort of web hovering over the entrance. I almost walked into it but instead did one of those awkward flinching maneuvers where everyone around you sees your body suddenly jerk to the side, but none of them can see *why,* thereby creating the impression that you are in some way impaired.

Web averted, I walked inside the store and felt there was something different about the place, something decidedly creepy. And then I saw what they really were. Not spider webs, but single strands hanging from the twenty-five-foot ceiling. Lizarraga occupies a space that looks like a warehouse, so the ceilings are high. These single strands hung down, and when I was brave enough to take a close look, I saw that each one had thousands of tiny caterpillars clinging to it. And there were hundreds of these strands hanging throughout the store. I wanted to bolt right then, but I struggle with irrational feelings of guilt if I enter a place and don't make a purchase. Like I've somehow caused more work for them with my presence and damn well better buy something in exchange. During road trips, I've been known to use a gas station restroom, then purchase something I really do not want or need, like Corn Nuts or control-top panty hose sold in a plastic silver egg, just to feel like it's been a fair trade.

I very carefully navigated my way around the creepy caterpillar strands and bought a bag of jalapeños, which is a vegetable that I only eat when it's filled with meat and cheese, which sort of defeats the purpose of my quest for healthier foods. Then again, jalapeños are, in fact, a vegetable.

A day later, I found one of the minuscule caterpillars creeping along my shoulder. The creature was so tiny that an ant would seem gigantic in comparison. I put the image of the millions of caterpillars from the produce store out of my head and viewed the creature in a new light. Anything small enough takes on a quality of cuteness, and I delicately transferred the being from shoulder to finger to palm tree, figuring this a suitable home. Over the next few days, I found the caterpillars on me regularly as they'd begun a full invasion of the town, and their presence went from cute to nuisance. My protective care turned to crushing them into nothingness between my fingers while yelling, *"Die, fucker!"* Nights were spent losing a war with insomnia, frantically scratching at my skin, trying to relieve the itching from bugs, some real and some imagined, crawling all over my body.

* * *

We were in Mexico for the second annual Todos Santos music festival. It's three weeks of concerts all over town, largely funded and organized by one of the members of REM. A few weeks before the festival began, we went to the opening of a new restaurant in Todos Santos called The Distillery. We were there, as well as Peter Buck, who my mother-in-law attempted to point out to us as "the guy from *rem.*"

"No, Mom," Mike corrected. "It's R-E-M, okay? You can't ever call it *rem* again, understand?"

Nana wasn't offended by this correction, as she'd much rather be corrected than eventually meet Peter Buck and blurt out, "Yes, you're the guy from *rem!*"

As the music festival approached, I felt my anxiety heighten a bit. It's one of those events that's supposed to be fun, and you know it will be fun, but you're just not sure if you're the right person for it. I'm not a music person. I hate to admit this because I often get the same reaction as when I admit that I'm not a dog person. But it's true. I'm just not a music person. I generally run about ten years behind in terms of what's out there. And it's not that I don't listen to music. I do. But if I have the option of silence, I choose silence. I like music as background at dinner parties and whatnot, but if I'm alone in the house and silence is an opportunity, I take it. I think that's fairly normal for most mothers of small children. We're so used to the television on and the constant repetition of Mom, Mom, Mom. Or the fighting and bickering and whining. Silence becomes truly golden in value.

The idea of going to a concert makes me anxious because I never know what to do with myself. Am I supposed to sing along? Jump up and down? Dance? Sit in a chair and lightly nod my head and tap my feet? I don't know and therefore end up feeling like a bit of a poser. The same way I'd feel if I went to church or tried to volunteer at the Humane Society. I've felt uncomfortable even at concerts featuring some of my favorite musicians. I've seen Bob Dylan, Tom Petty, Santana, and the Violent Femmes, the commonality of these groups being that they prove I am no longer young. Even when you get to see a star up close, they're still just people. They have the same appendages, skin issues, and blue jeans that the rest of us have. A friend of mine took me to see Josh Ritter, who I like very much. He had backstage passes and offered one of them to me, but I declined and opted to give it to someone else. Because if I got to meet Josh Ritter, what would I say? "Good job. Good singing out there tonight. That was really spot on." I don't even want to meet celebrities that I'm a fan of because the most that would happen is I'd make a fool of myself and have a new memory to cringe over every time it entered my insecure little brain.

The music festival meant that town was crowded, the streets were loud, and if anyone were to end up tripping and breaking their nose on the sidewalk or getting pickpocketed, I would inevitably be that person. What I like about Todos Santos is that it's a sleepy little town. So to me, a time when everyone is going to an event is a perfect time to stay home, get drunk, and watch a movie. But I don't want to give license to the whiny homebody that lurks deep inside, and when I do venture out, I usually enjoy myself. Everyone else was going, and we had a babysitter, so I had to bury all of my anxieties, not give in to the temptation to feign uncontrollable diarrhea, and have a good time.

We had tickets to attend three of the concerts during the three-week period of the festival. On the day of the first one, I was exhausted. But maybe this had more to do with my anxiety about going than with actual physical exhaustion. The night before, Mike and I had collapsed into bed as soon as we got the girls to sleep, which means we went to bed at 8:35 p.m. I yawned throughout the day and dreaded the evening. When we finally went, it was at Hotel California. As in, "livin' it up at the Hotel California." Apparently, Todos Santos was the inspiration for that song. Although across the street is Tequila Sunrise, which boasts that it's the *real* Hotel California. A bit of a feud extends back and forth across the street, but honestly, we're talking about the Eagles from 1977. At this point, I don't think anyone really gives a shit.

At Hotel California, Peter Buck, the member of REM, was playing with his band. I was fairly indifferent to the music, although the more drinks I had, the better it sounded. Then the band got off the stage and made way for the next act. A short, bald man got up and began singing familiar songs that were popular the year I graduated from high school. The more he sang, the more people began looking around at each other and saying, "Wow, he sure sounds a lot like the real guy." And it was the real guy, though we all knew the name of the band, Live, but no one knew the name of the singer, which I later found out is Ed. His last name includes the letters k, c, z, and w, which means I automatically give up on ever trying to pronounce it.

Elizabeth stood next to me. "Oh my gosh, I can't believe it's the real guy. I mean, these songs meant so much to me," she said. Elizabeth is unquestionably earnest when she makes statements like these, though you also get the feeling that there are probably a few hundred singers that she would say the same thing about.

He finished his songs and exited the stage.

"Well, go tell him that," I encouraged. "Go on, be a groupie."

"Do you think I should?" she asked.

"Yes, you know you're going to regret it if you don't."

"Yeah, but I don't even know the guy's name," she said.

"That's okay. Just go up to him and tell him what you told me, about how those songs mean a lot to you."

"Okay, I'll do it." Elizabeth went up to the singer to express her admiration.

Later in the evening, the guy walked by us.

"It's him!" I said, and I reached out and tapped him on the shoulder as he passed.

He stopped and turned to me, waiting for me to say something. But then I realized that I really had nothing to say. He stood waiting, and all eyes in the group were on me. I understood now the awkwardness Elizabeth had referred to in complimenting someone whose name you don't even know. And it's not even that the person ever has to know that you don't know their name. People often don't use other people's names in the course of normal conversation, but just being aware that you have this gaping hole where knowledge should be is disconcerting. I was drunk by this point, and the crowd continued to stare. Maybe I thought someone else was going to jump in. I think because our entire group was so impressed with this man, I thought that I was doing everyone a favor by getting his attention, and then the rest of the people could say whatever it is they had a burning desire to say. But Elizabeth had already spoken to him, and apparently no one else felt the need to elaborate any further. The man waited, but I could tell he was sizing up my mental capabilities. Then I just mumbled, "I… uh… well… just… uh…" I fell silent, and he walked away.

"Wow, Amanda, that was really something." Elizabeth smiled. "I honestly don't think you could have blown that one any worse."

"She does that with celebrities," Mike chimed in. "I've seen it before."

Later in the evening, the singer's promoter walked by our group. "We want to buy him a drink," I said, hoping to somehow make up for my previous idiocy. This, too, is a stupid offering. There is no way that the featured act has to pay for his own drinks. The singer never returned, but we chatted with the promoter for a while. He had dark, curly hair that I couldn't help but stare at. Every now and then, I meet a man with hair that turns me into Lenny from *Of Mice and Men.* It just looks so dark, soft, and wonderful that I have to touch it. And when I'm drunk, this seems like a good idea. So, in the middle of normal party conversation, I reached up and began running my fingers through his hair. This isn't a sexy, seductive sort of move; it's more like I'm entranced by it and can't help but reach out and touch it, reminiscent of Ivy's behavior toward her blankie. She likes to touch it because it's there and it's soft. Somewhere in the back of my mind, I knew that stroking a stranger's head meant that it was time for me to leave.

* * *

After the town had collectively recovered from the music festival, my in-laws hosted a party, and I found myself chatting with Tim, the neighbor.

"You know," he said, "it's like in the sixties, because I was the right age at the right time. It was LSD and introspection. You know?"

"Uh... yeah." I nodded.

"But then people began showing up for the party, and the party was over. If you showed up for the party, you didn't get it. You know?"

"Right." I nodded again.

"But if you showed up, and you were ready to look inside, then you were rewarded. And *you* are definitely ready."

He was so difficult to follow that at one point I gave up trying to understand and just focused on when the story would end. I couldn't figure out what he was telling me I was ready for. Possibly LSD or introspection or a party, or maybe all of those were really the same thing.

"You know what I'm saying?" he asked.

"Yes." I did not.

At that point, he held up his full margarita and pressed it to my face. I'm not sure if he wanted to put a hand on my cheek and forgot that he was holding a drink, or if I was supposed to gain some sort of inner peace and knowledge that would flow from within him, through his arm, through the margarita, and into my face. He didn't just touch the glass to my face and then put it down; he held it there in place and stared at me with a slight smile.

Eventually I felt compelled to speak. "Um, that's really cold," I said. He continued pressing the glass to my face, which was beginning to numb. "I think I hear a kid crying somewhere. I better go and see if it's one of mine."

He relented and withdrew. "Fine, you're free, you're free," he said, realizing that I wanted out of the conversation. I went to mingle with others and was glad for the cover of darkness. Surely the right side of my face was bright red from the cold. I may also have had a few stray grains of salt clinging to my cheek from the rim of his glass. In the light of day, people would probably think I'd either fallen and landed on the side of my face, or that someone had slapped me. I was happy for the interaction, though. It eased my embarrassment over having stroked the head of a stranger at the music festival. We all have our moments.

* * *

CHAPTER SEVENTEEN

Circus in Town

People assumed that living in Mexico for three months implied a glamorous life. We'd come a long way from the days of the luxury poop bucket, but we were an equally long way from glamorous. While I love to travel, I was ready for comfort. I looked forward to using my gym membership and shopping at the store and making fabulous meals in my own kitchen. I wanted to again feel competent in my ability to put gas in the car without being swindled, an unfortunate but common occurrence at the downtown Todos Santos gas station, and to know that my children could use the bathroom without encountering a scorpion in the process. I was ready to dress from a closet full of clothes instead of a suitcase, to allow my kids to brush their teeth with water from the bathroom sink, and to make use of the modern marvel that is a garbage disposal.

We bade farewell to the Todos Santos community, to the Montessori school, to friends who'd thrown parties and had us over for dinner. We said goodbye to Tim and Melissa and returned the keys to the Monster Truck with great thanks. We had a final farewell with Chris and Elizabeth and their beautiful children. We shared a last meal with Nana and Papa and attempted to communicate our thanks for all they continue to do for us. The goodbye wasn't difficult, as our trips to Todos Santos have become annual events, so "goodbye" turns into "see you next year."

Nana drove us to the airport, and we began the trek back to Idaho. It's a full day of travel that I've come to think of as Dear God Is It Over Yet. But each year as our kids grow older, travel becomes a little easier. They understand the processes of checking bags and changing planes, and they require less bribery to get through them than when they were infants and toddlers. After blissfully uneventful stops in San Diego and Seattle, we arrived home at midnight, tired but otherwise intact. When we entered our home, the girls grew excited despite the late hour.

"I remember this house," said Emilia.

"I remember these toys," said Ivy.

We put them to bed and hauled our suitcases into the house.

"All I want to find is a toothbrush and toothpaste," I said. "That's all I care about." We located these and brushed our teeth, but I then became aware of a disgusting but familiar feeling after a full day of travel—like someone had slathered my face in lard.

"I lied," I admitted. "I also need to find a bar of soap. After I wash my face, that's really all I care about." This proved more difficult than I would have anticipated. I searched the house to find that not a single bar of soap existed. I found liquid hand soap and used that instead. Finally, Mike and I got into bed.

"Holy crap," Mike said. "Was our bed always this comfortable?"

"I have no idea," I responded. "I can't talk right now, though. It's just too good."

Despite the comfort of my own, cockroach-free bed after three months away, I held a momentary fear that I would have difficulty going to sleep. There were huge suitcases to unpack the next day, mountains of laundry to do, and bars of soap to purchase. Would my car even start in the morning? Would we return to Todos Santos for a full three months the next winter? People had asked us the last question repeatedly as our time in Mexico came to a close, but we didn't yet have an answer.

* * *

In our first week back, Mike and I found ourselves scrambling to catch up with our former lives, while Emilia and Ivy went right back into their prior routines without a hitch, save for a slight setback in Emilia's Mandarin proficiency when compared with the rest of her class. I wasn't overly concerned with her having fallen behind; just having a healthy, happy five-year-old was good enough for me. And surely after the summer, the students would be on a level playing field again, in any case. The most important issues to Emilia upon our return were being reunited with Charlie and her first loose tooth. Every minute, both at school and at home, was spent showing off the tooth to anyone willing to peer into her open mouth.

When the tooth came out, the tooth fairy, who may have been intoxicated at the time, gave Emilia a dollar bill along with a few peso coins. The next morning, she emerged from her room distraught and tearfully cried, "This is the worst day of my whole entire life! The tooth fairy didn't come!"

"What are you talking about?" said Mike. "Of course the tooth fairy came."

"No she didn't. Look," she commanded, and held up her tooth, which the drunken tooth fairy had forgotten to remove from beneath her pillow.

"Oh," said Mike. "Maybe she just decided that you get to keep your tooth. Let's go have another look."

He walked her back to her room and showed her that the tooth fairy had indeed paid her a visit, a dollar, and *seis* pesos. "Wow," she said. "This is the best day of my whole entire life!"

On the evening of the best day of her whole entire life, we had family over for dinner. "Shaka-kahn, how was Mexico?" Virgil asked.

"It was great," Mike answered.

"Man, I need a vacation. I can't even remember the last time I was there."

"Virgil," I interrupted, "you got *married* the last time you went to Mexico."

"Oh. I guess you're right. But it only lasted six months, so that doesn't really count. But I really do need a vacation. I just need to take some time to sit and relax. I've been so stressed lately."

"Have you been working a lot?" I asked.

"No. I need a job."

"Uncle Virgil, look at my tooth," Emilia interrupted, holding it up for him to see.

"Wow, that's… creepy."

Sandi and Matt arrived along with Bella and Rosie.

"Uncle Matt, look at my tooth," Emilia said, trying to elicit a better response than the one she'd received from Uncle Virgil.

"Good job, Emilia. First tooth gone!" he said. "But I'm going to have to ask that you refer to me as *Handsome* Uncle Matt from now on."

"Handsome Uncle Matt. Got it," said Emilia.

"I want a name like that," said Virgil.

"You changed your name to Virgil," said Matt. "You don't get to add anything else to it."

"I don't mean to be rude," I interjected, "but I want you all to get out of my kitchen." Both children and adults dutifully obeyed and moved to the backyard.

By far one of the biggest rewards in returning to Boise was taking possession of my own kitchen. My kitchen is my domain, my Zen, my happy place, my realm of comfort and control. I take great joy in feeding others, making sure this one component of basic survival is not only met, but met well. When Mike and I first met, I could barely make toast. He did much of the cooking early on, and it quickly became apparent to me that I would need to acquire some level of proficiency in the kitchen.

"Are you trying to help me lose weight?" I asked when he presented me with a teaspoonful of scrambled eggs.

"What are you talking about?"

"This is not a breakfast," I complained.

"Well, you're a girl, so you don't need as much," he said. In the thirteen years since, he's learned that I'm quite capable of gluttony, and on the rare occasion when he prepares a meal, he gives me as much food as my fat ass desires.

When dinner was ready, I allowed everyone back.

"We're having risotto?" Virgil said. "Awesome. Hand me the Tabasco." We watched as Virgil ruined a perfect risotto by drenching it in hot sauce. "I thought we were having steak," he said.

"No one ever said anything about steak," I responded. "Why would you think we were having steak?"

"Maybe I was just thinking of that story Dad likes to tell, the one where you stabbed his hand with a fork because you wanted the biggest steak for yourself."

"That story is *not* true," I insisted.

Papa had joined Mike and me for dinner the previous summer. We had steak. It was only the three of us, so there were three steaks. They were all large. It wasn't like there was an imbalance, as if two of the steaks were sizable and one puny. They were all big steaks, all similar.

When we sat down to eat, I abandoned my usual practice of letting the men indulge in their caveman behavior before filling my own plate. I was tired of caveman behavior. I dealt with caveman behavior all the time. I was ready for a little ladies-first behavior. So I helped myself. I put a steak on my plate, added some veggies, and sat down to eat. This is what the men do. They don't wait or serve others, so why should I not do the same, I reasoned. Since that night, my father-in-law has relished telling the story of when we sat down to eat and I took the biggest steak for myself. He's prone to exaggeration, so over time, the story has evolved into him reaching for the biggest steak and me stabbing his hand with my fork in an effort to stop him.

"Why does that story get you so riled up?" Sandi asked.

"Because it's not true. Because I spend a ridiculous chunk of my life feeding other people and making sure they get the biggest and best portion of everything. Because I pride myself on table manners, and your father, who has quite a different code of conduct when it comes to food, likes to tell this story that makes me sound like a pig."

There was a moment of silence before Matt quietly said, "Methinks she doth protest too much."

"That's it," I said. "I'm never calling you Handsome Matt again."

"I think it's funny," said Sandi.

"Plus, I don't want my daughters growing up thinking that there's any truth to a story of me stabbing Papa during an altercation over food," I added. "Or me stabbing Papa at all."

After dinner, Bella did Emilia's hair, which involved putting as many barrettes, bows, clips, and hair bands onto Emilia's head as was humanly possible. Rosie practiced her cartwheels and attempted to instruct Ivy in the execution of a perfect cartwheel, though the end result was just Ivy bending over with her hands on the ground and her butt stuck up in the air. This move was also accompanied by Ivy's commentary of, "Hey, Rosie, look at my bum-bum."

When Emilia's hair was "done" and the cartwheel lesson complete, all four girls decided to try on leotards. Both Bella and Rosie have done their fair share of gymnastics and over the years accumulated a ridiculous amount of leotards. This is good, as apparently they are expensive, and I have a built-in system of hand-me-downs so that I don't have to spend the money on them.

Bella and Rosie had reached the age where they'd suddenly grown in height and thinned out as a result. Emilia was beginning to enter this stage, while Ivy wasn't there yet and still had the sort of cheeks and legs and arms that you can't help but squeeze. I can't say that I wasn't a little jealous of Ivy's status. If chubby cheeks and dimpled thighs were as attractive on adults as they are on three-year-olds, I'd be set. So when all four girls presented themselves to the room with a grand ta-da and struck a pose, it was a mix of grace, strength, awkwardness, and protruding bellies. And when I say leotards, I'm not talking about the plain black that they had when I was a kid. These leotards included American flags, pink crushed velvet, and neon leopard print.

"Okay, now everyone go to the backyard," Rosie commanded. "It's time for the circus."

The circus involves all of the adults sitting as the audience while the children demonstrate various skits and talents. Anything goes, and this particular circus included Emilia twirling a plastic shovel, Rosie playing both parts in a story about a man and his zebra, Bella doing back handsprings, and Ivy throwing shoes at her cousins.

"I love the circus," whispered Sandi.

"Me, too," I agreed as Ivy finished a beautiful rendition of the ABC song and brought the performance to a close.

"So you had a great time in Mexico?" she asked.

"We did. At the same time, I'm really glad we're back. It feels good to be home."

"Do you think you'll do another three-month trip?"

"Maybe," I answered. "But right now I'm pretty content here. And I'm pretty content with this." I gestured to the girls in their leotards, to their unabashed devotion to anything silly.

She held her glass to mine, and we clinked. It was the sound of boxed wine in cheap glasses against the backdrop of giggling children. And it was perfect.

* * *

If you enjoyed this book, please consider posting
a review online. If you did not enjoy this book,
eat chocolate because that will make you feel better.

*A.K. Turner is available for speaking engagements,
writers conferences, book clubs, email banter, or a glass of wine.
Visit AKTurner.com or email her at amanda@AKTurner.com.*

The following people are awesome: Elizabeth Day,
Laurie Notaro, Cameron Morfit, Holand Peterson, Eric Stoffle,
Kristen Lynch, Robin O'Bryant, Elaine Ambrose,
Stacy Dymalski, Sarah Tregay, my in-laws, teachers,
cab drivers, good bartenders, and all of the wonderful readers who
have taken the time to review my work or to let me know they
enjoyed it. And enormous thanks to my husband,
who deserves a hell of a lot more than a little thank you
at the end of this book.

2/14

CPSIA information can be obtained at www.ICGtesting.com
Printed in the USA
LVOW12s1439210114

370364LV00017B/547/P

9 780985 583989